Psychotherapy

The Private and Very Personal Viewpoints of Doctor and Patient

Harold E. McNeely, Ph.D

The Private and Very Persona

nd Norma Taylor Obele

Psychotherapy

Viewpoints of Doctor and Patient

Nelson-Hall Company Chicago

ISBN: 0-911012-35-4

Library of Congress Catalog Card Number: 72-88581

Manufactured in the United States of America

Although the examples in this book are based on the behavior of real people, the names have been changed, along with other significant biographical information, to protect the identity of persons living or dead.

Preface

This book is directed toward all those readers who are interested in the workings of the human mind and heart, particularly those who are now, have been, or plan to be involved in some form of psychotherapy. It is addressed to the husband or wife who is sometimes bewildered by his or her spouse's behavior after a session with the therapist; to the psychotherapy patient who worries about his progress and who wonders what happens to other patients during their treatment; and, finally, to the person who occasionally feels that he is "losing his mind," but who fears he would sound silly or ridiculous if he were to express his anxieties to another person.

We were prompted to embark upon the project of writing this book because we feel that the process of psychotherapy is still unnecessarily shrouded in a cloak of mystery. While many current books, movies, and television shows deal with the subject, too often the therapist is presented as a problem-free, calm, cool, all-knowing superbachelor, and the client is portrayed as the distraught, befuddled, ineffectual patient in the therapeutic situation. Seldom is the relationship portrayed as it should be, that is, as one in which two people are engaged in a helpful partnership.

We have chosen to present this case history in story form, since most people like to read stories better than they do dry, technical books. Our aim is to acquaint the reader in an enjoyable and readable form with the intimate workings of psychotherapy. We hope to satisfy the reader's curiosity not only about the psychotherapy patient, but also about the psychotherapist. What do they really discuss in the inner sanctum? How do they both feel about his patients? Why will people reveal themselves in therapy more than they will at home? Do the therapist's own feelings ever affect the treatment? Finally, how much lasting change occurs in the patient and how close can he come to accepting himself as he is? These are questions we hope to answer in the following pages.

The unique feature of the book is a marked emphasis on the private thoughts, feelings, and day dreams of the therapist as well as those of the patient. His history and background are revealed in addition to the patient's. This technique is employed not to minimize the professional therapist nor to make him an antihero, but rather to humanize him. It is our feeling that the psychotherapist can accomplish a great deal more with his patients by being an open and real person than by acting as a silent and impassive sounding board.

CHAPTER 1

As his next to last patient of the day walked out the rear door, Dr. R. Ross Odell breathed a heavy sigh and sagged back in his chair. His deep concentration with his patient this last hour had completely suspended any feelings of fatigue, but now he was alone and he felt relieved that there was only one hour left to work and that that hour was with a particularly enjoyable patient, Helen James.

He took a quick look at his appointment book because when he got exceptionally tired at the end of the day, he sometimes confused days of the week. It was always a shock to him to walk into the small waiting room expecting to see one patient only to find another. In addition he was not very good at hiding his feelings so his patient usually saw the shocked expression. In his earlier years as a therapist he had lied or evaded the truth of his confusion to avoid feeling embarrassed over such a seemingly ridiculous incompetence. Then either he or the patient or both had felt stiff, uncomfortable, or ill at ease—feelings hardly conducive to psychotherapy which rests so heavily on trust.

He had ignored the problem until a paranoid male patient whom he really liked had suddenly quit and never returned after such a "confusion" in the waiting room. He had both called the patient on the telephone and written him a letter telling the truth, but it had been too late for this suspicious, untrusting man who could give only one chance to anyone. It still troubled Dr. Odell, particularly since he liked the man, to think that his own defensiveness had helped keep another human secretive, closed, unhappy, narrow-minded, and lonely. It relieved him to remember that an older therapist had once said, "Even a good therapist loses one patient for each important thing he learns."

He got up suddenly, realizing that it was five o'clock, and he hadn't heard the click of the waiting room door. Helen might be in the waiting room, but he doubted it because he nearly always heard the outer door with its distinctive click. He opened the thick, insulated door to find he was correct—no Helen yet. He left the door open, expecting her any second as she had been prompt for a long time.

Idly thinking his wrist watch might be wrong, he looked at his new desk clock, a handsome Mexican clock given to him by his wife, Nora, on his forty-first birthday last week. He knew she had made a special trip to Nogales, Mexico, to get the hand carved clock after not being able to find the right one in Phoenix. He realized she had taken their three children along, since their birthday presents had been an assortment of hand carved items from Mexico. His family knew he was currently a nut on wood carvings.

Where was Helen? She was over ten minutes late now, and she hadn't been that late in six months, even with two appointments a week. His first thought was that she might have car trouble, as she seemed to have more mysterious, undiagnosed ailments in her car than anyone else he knew. He had a vague momentary fear that she might have had a car accident, but dismissed that thought. Then he began to try to recall what had happened in her last hour. He couldn't remember anything significant. She had been coming to psychotherapy twice a week for over two years and wasn't too far away from finishing treatment. They had a steady, proven relationship now after a hectic, stormy first year of therapy. Maybe he had become overconfident and too relaxed so he had missed some subtle signs of distress. He couldn't really imagine a serious flaw in their relationship.

If Helen's lateness proved sufficiently significant, he would bring up this situation at the next weekly meeting of his countertransference group. With this thought, he immediately felt more relaxed and confident. It was reassuring to have a therapy group for therapists from whom he could get really good help for these more uncomfortable relationships with patients. He knew he could rely on the other five therapists in his group either to help him identify and resolve the hidden part of this problem or to reassure him that he was over-reading the possible significance of this tardiness. He thought about his group for a moment and hoped that Jeff, a fellow psychologist, wouldn't be too big a bastard this week and sabotage his need for help. While Jeff was a highly trained and skilled psychotherapist, he could still be a real pain in the neck. He guessed that Jeff would stop being obnoxious, argumentative, and self-centered if he really pressed to get the group focused on his problem with Helen.

He again sank back in his high-backed, well-padded chair. Maybe something simple and straightforward had happened to Helen like a late but urgent request for immediate work from her boss—or an important and lengthy long distance phone call for her at the last minute. He could remember the time early in therapy when Helen seemed to have a relentless, interminable battle with time so that she was chronically late despite her best efforts. He had never heard such lengthy and convincing excuses for lateness as she could provide. He had even started to look forward to her next original alibi.

She did not cease being late until he bought a small chalk blackboard and silently wrote down both her previous total and her waste of time that day in terms of her own calculation: "Yes, sixty cents a minute, that's what it costs me to be late." She had laughed at his blackboard at first, but she slowly reduced her lateness when the blackboard total rose above $100. She was expert with words and would have talked away the significance of her lateness if he had argued or discussed time with her. Her sarcasm, pouting, stubbornness, and denials did not change the ever increasing amount on the silent blackboard.

Finally one day she had become really angry with him over the blackboard and had called him "a cold, uninvolved, time-pinching computer who was trying to break her spirit with seconds and minutes." Her outburst of anger had served to release her from the childlike position that he, the parent-therapist, was forcing her to conform to his time demands and that the most she could do was to rebel by being late. She then realized that she did not have to be either the conforming child who comes on time or the rebelling child who is always late, but that she could be, if she wished, a true adult who chooses to make agreements about time with another adult and to use her own time in the most effective way. She now laughed with him about her "$100 lesson."

He had found Helen sexually attractive even in her first hour. Even though her stocky body had never fit the more slender and curvaceous model of American beauty, her rapid walk and erect carriage had seemed to promise an active and enthusiastic roll in the hay. Her long brown hair looked full and luxuriant, and she had a mouth with full lips and a substantial nose with a slight Roman curve that somehow accented the promise of sensuality. She complained to him that her brown eyes were "too close set" and that her eyebrows were "bushes if I don't work on them," but she was her own worst critic and had no real basis for complaint.

For a long time she had remained quite oblivious to

her own attractiveness, and his occasional compliment was ignored or never acknowledged. The closest she could come to favorable self-appraisal was to agree that her hands both looked and were efficient and well coordinated—this admission having to be followed by comments that her feet were "lumps" and that one ear was slightly higher than the other. He recalled vaguely his notes from the first hour, describing her as a "well-developed, well-nourished, slightly obese, but attractive brunette with bold features and compact, short-armed, short-legged build, apparently of energetic nature with a rapid walk and fast speech."

Having reminded himself of his early impressions of Helen, he reached into his drawer containing files on current patients and pulled her chart. He quickly scanned the family history and a letter from her family doctor and then came to the results of her psychological tests. He reread the report as he had not reviewed it for some time.

Irving Steinberg, M.D.
4925 North Saguaro Lane
Phoenix, Arizona

Re: JAMES, Mrs. Helen
Dear Irv:
I am genuinely sorry to be writing this letter to you. It is bad enough to be confessing my apparent ineptness with a patient who now transfers to you, but also she is an intelligent, attractive, anxious woman who both appealed to me personally and will prob-

ably make a very good patient. I guess I came on "too strong" with her, frightened her away by being over-eager with the psychological test results. She canceled the next appointment after I had interpreted the test results to her. I was so anxious to help her immediately and impress her with my fast understanding of her that I told her too much. I did call her the next week, but she was very brusque and businesslike, saying, "I have arranged to see someone else. I've sent you a signed release for a report. Thank you." Well, good luck, and don't try to go too fast or move in on her.

Here are the results of my psychological testing —"the testing was a splendid success but the patient transferred." I saw her for four hours of testing plus sending a couple of tests along with her to do at home. The following tests were administered to her: (1) Rorschach Test, (2) Wechsler Adult Intelligence Scale, (3) Thematic Apperception Test, (4) Minnesota Multiphasic Personality Inventory, (5) Sentence Completion Test, (6) Bender Gestalt Test, and (7) Draw-A-Person Test.

The general diagnostic impression was formed of a highly anxious but well-integrated woman of superior intelligence who fits roughly into the hysterical category. There is a second possibility that her problems are of characterological proportions, in which case she may function like an overcompensated oral character with massive defenses against repressed dependency needs. She obviously requires delicate handling but has a good prognosis for both short-term and long-term psychotherapy.

There were no signs of an overt or underlying psychosis or psychotic tendencies. No significant evidence was seen along brain injury or minimal brain damage lines. She has some depressive potential with mild suicidal ideation but is not very likely to make a serious attempt. Her anxiety level is high enough to motivate her for psychotherapy. She should have a male therapist as she has even less trust of females than her substantial mistrust of males. Boy, are you going to have to prove yourself to this woman!

In more detail as to her intelligence, she obtained a W.A.I.S. IQ of 126, getting nearly equal scores on the verbal and the performance sections. Basically she functions very adequately in the intellectual sphere. She is well informed, efficient, reasonable, observant, and shows good judgment in intellectual tasks. Her hysterical tendencies are shown in her mild histrionics, occasional exaggerations, and lapses into superficiality. Surprisingly for this kind of woman, she demonstrates excellent ability to handle very detailed work, suggesting a substantial degree of compulsiveness under the more flippant, casual veneer. She shows good usage of her capacities for practical, daily problems of living. Her deficiency is in her inability to bring about an integration of broad organization in her personal, emotional life.

In broad perspective she sees reality with good accuracy. She never distorts in a psychotic way. Her thought processes assume conventional channels. In fact, she is overconventionalized, quite ruled and bound by standard morality and overconsideration for the rights of other people. She has a wealth of affectual resources and a really good capacity for mutually satisfying, reciprocal relationships with other people; however, she now fears her own emotionality and distrusts her ability to make appropriate discriminations between her friends and her enemies. She has a deep-seated feeling of inferiority which is partly compensated for by an attitude of superiority. She has a very active fantasy life and a good potential for introspection. She can imagine people in a great variety of roles but keeps them at a distance from herself. She shows a strong tendency toward a neurotic withdrawal from people when she feels threatened, either by too much closeness or pressure.

A major problem involves her unacceptable dependency feelings. She can tolerate and may even encourage others to depend on her, but she is extremely fearful and suspicious about depending on or really trusting anyone else. She is primarily unaware of her strong need or desire to receive "unconditional" love from another person, probably from a kindly, benevolent, understanding parental figure.

She cannot accept her more childlike feelings. Her ego ideal is far more that of a very adequate, independent, self-sufficient, accomplishing, progressing person. She does have tremendous drive and energy—accomplishing a great deal even though her efforts are motivated defensively to prove inexhaustible or limitless productivity. She is not capable of receiving much from others, but she can give a great amount and partially identify with the recipient of her own giving. It must be easy for her friends or family or even acquaintances to manipulate her, to convince her to be a supermother who gives all and asks nothing in return.

As expected, she has real trouble with anger. She refuses to admit the depth of her angry, frustrated feelings besides being more directly repressed in the whole area of aggressive feelings. Hostility from others, as well as her own angry impulses, serves as a real threat to her. It is difficult for her to say "no" to anyone, no matter how unreasonable the request, since her refusal might engender hostile reactions. She thinks of arguments and squabbles as serious rejections and does not recognize the real need for some angry exchange in a mature relationship.

She does have a need to have everyone love her. Her depression probably originates from her turning her anger back on herself and blaming herself rather than having appropriate, normal expressions of anger. Her suppression and repression of anger are also in protection of her dependency needs—more specifically a holding in of anger with the hope of getting love or keeping love coming from a parent figure. She will need support, approval and acceptance before she becomes proficient in expression of angry feelings.

She appears to have made a feminine identification although her concept is of the masochistic, nurturing, self-sacrificing woman. She appears to have identified with a mother figure who is reluctantly serving, self-sufficient, miserably committed to a dull, routine life and stodgy husband. Her mother figure is self-sacrificing, giving, and dutiful on the surface, but ungiving, guilt-producing, and subtly punishing at a deeper level. She perceives her father at the top level as a strong but quiet, shy, stubborn, undemonstrative man who loved her. At a deeper level she sees him as a weak, dependent, rigid man who is lovable but quite blind as to her real needs. She can love and serve a man, but she doesn't really even hope that a man could love her, perceive her needs, and satisfy her. She has probably picked a husband with conspicuous similarities to her father, with just enough differences to be quite defensible to her.

Here are a few odds and ends I haven't tucked into place. She does indulge in some rather clever magical solutions, such as half believing that her car will heal itself if she lets it sit. She constantly fights time and money, keeping herself under maximum pressure.

To hell with it. I'm too long-winded. Call me if you want to discuss anything more.

Sincerely yours,
R. Ross Odell, Ph.D.
Clinical Psychologist

He closed the chart and put it back in the files in his desk. He felt happy now that he had had a good reason to dictate a report on Helen. He hated dictating reports. Over the years he had lost numerous good referral sources by procrastinating in sending reports to the referring physicians. He had almost forgotten he had this report on Helen. It was hard to remember now that she had left treatment temporarily and had gone to see Irving Steinberg.

He smiled now, remembering how she had returned to him after one session with Steinberg. She had told him, stating the truth as if it were a joke, "My God! You were bad enough—with all your mumbo jumbo about those tests. But that Dr. Steinberg! He made me feel like a bug on a pin. Never has an hour gone so slow! He sat there like a pompous demigod stroking that analyst's beard of his and staring at me. Do you know I have never seen anyone in my life— even in the movies—who looked more like a psychoanalyst? It was terrifying. With that little clipped beard and the Jewish name and the German accent, he made me feel like an absolute nut. I could hardly tell the man my name. He made me feel sick, I mean really sick. Who else but a sickie would require the services of Freud himself? Now don't get smug and think I like any of this business. But at least with you I feel as if I'm sort of chatting with my old Irish friend about my troubles. If it is possible to be comfortable in such a situation as this—and I doubt it—you are the lesser of two evils."

Dr. Odell had felt this was a pretty left-handed compliment and was rather dubious about her stated reasons for selecting him, but he was content to let her come, whatever her reasons.

He looked again at his watch and wished Helen would arrive. However, his own magical thinking had failed him and she did not appear at his desire.

Chapter 2

As Dr. Odell waited for Helen, she was making her way to his office through the evening traffic. (Damn it! How could I have forgotten this is Thursday?) She still had nearly five miles of heavy Phoenix traffic to cross to get to his office as the announcer on her car radio declared it to be five o'clock. Each time she had to stop for a red light she took it as a personal affront. At that moment she unreasoningly hated every other driver on the road.

Weaving in and out of traffic and gunning her car every time a slight opening appeared ahead, she was ticking off the minutes in terms of money. (Don't these damn fools know this is costing me sixty cents a minute!) At the beginning of her therapy she had figured out the fee per minute, and for several hours afterward had found it difficult to converse with Dr. Odell because of the meter that was running in her head clicking off the thirty dollars for the session. (Well, it's my money, isn't it? I earn it, don't I? If I'm late nobody suffers but me.) Nonetheless, she knew

the first thing Dr. Odell would do would be to make
her deal with her tardiness today. She would then
have to confess to him that she had completely forgotten it was time for her Thursday appointment until Tom Perry, the lawyer for whom she worked, had
come into her office and had been surprised to see her
still there, thinking she had already left. She felt a
great deal of warmth for Tom and was grateful to
him for the support he had given her during the last
two years while she had been in treatment. He had
consistently encouraged her to continue, letting her
off work half an hour early twice a week—today even
reminding her to leave.

"And that is the news to this hour," the radio
newsman announced. (Five minutes past five! Damn!
I'm going to be fifteen minutes late. Today of all days
when my marriage seems to be crumbling, and I
really need to talk to that doctor.) All day she had
pushed last night's bitter words with Steve out of her
mind. Apparently she was still doing so by "forgetting" her appointment to prolong the avoidance.

Maybe Dr. Odell wouldn't even wait for her.
Since she was the last patient for the day, he had probably already locked his office and gone home. He was
doubtless delighted that she hadn't shown up and had
an excuse not to see her today. Right now he most
likely was entering the front door of his house where
his gorgeous wife (whom Helen had never seen) had
drinks mixed and was waiting for him. Said wife no
doubt was wearing glamorous, seductive lounging
pajamas and had a delicious dinner waiting in the

oven, and he was telling her how nice it was when his five o'clock patient didn't show up. Maybe his wife was sending the children out to play so they could have a quick tumble in bed before she served him the exotic dish she had cooked so carefully. (And I will be paying for the hour because I didn't call to cancel! By God!) The thought was too much that she should be put in a position of paying for his sex life. She already thought too much about what he might be like in the bedroom.

At this thought she began to smile to herself, realizing that she was thinking along the lines she had when she had first begun treatment. For all her mental histrionics, she knew that Dr. Odell would be patiently waiting for her. Nonetheless, she continued to feel a twinge of anger towards him as she maneuvered through the traffic.

It was 5:15 when she arrived at the doctor's office. As she pulled into the parking lot, she distinctly heard a "funny noise" under the hood of her car. She owned a four-year-old Lincoln Continental on which she was still making payments, feeling guilty at the amount each month when she wrote the check to the bank. Her husband, Steve, had protested the Lincoln as an unnecessary extravagance, but had backed off when she barraged him with a combination of female tears, cold logic, and barbed remarks that she would be working and paying for it and therefore it was "her business." He had unhappily capitulated, and while she enjoyed the car, she felt guilty about it and never mentioned any of its ailments to Steve. The idea of any additional expense for repairs was unthinkable to her.

Even though she knew she was already fifteen minutes late, she sat in the car and let the engine idle while she listened to the mysterious "click-click-thud" which hadn't been there a few minutes before. (The damned car is sick, too. The Lincoln mechanic doesn't know any more about fixing cars than that know-it-all headshrinker knows about fixing my head.) Deciding there was nothing she could do about it now, she climbed out of the car.

Still pondering over what new ailment her car had developed, she hurried with fast little clicking steps toward the rest room at the back of the office building. She felt harried, late, and frustrated, and the significance of heading in the opposite direction of Dr. Odell's office did not occur to her. It had become a ritual during her months of therapy to use this public rest room before each session. She never failed to arrive for her appointment in need of the plumbing facilities, and she also felt it imperative to comb her hair, redo her lipstick, and enter his office looking "neat, efficient, unharried, and invulnerable," no matter how inefficient and harried she had to be to accomplish the feat.

Helen had long ago admitted the twice-weekly ritual to Dr. Odell. When he had suggested that she could save time and trouble—and sixty cents a minute—by using his rest room right next to his office, the thought had horrified her. He might be able to sit in his office and listen to her tinkling away. While she was able to explain to him why she could not stand the thought of performing such bodily functions with only a well separating her from him, she was never able to change her ways. Thus it did not seem the least incongruous to her at 5:15 to be heading in the opposite direction from his office.

In the rest room she hurriedly powdered her nose and redid her mouth. She ran a comb through her hair while sitting on the john, feeling that this combination of effort was saving time and money. She made an effort to remember why she had been so eager to talk to Dr. Odell today. The reason for her haste seemed to have vanished; only the sense of hurry remained. Grabbing her purse and thrusting her comb, lipstick, and compact into it, she took off toward the doctor's office.

Chapter 3

Helen's heels clicked furiously on the tile as she hurried down the hall to Dr. Odell's office. Seeing his waiting room door open, she felt relief that he was still there and all her rushing and frustration had not been in vain.

For a moment she remembered other occasions early in her therapy when she had been late—a habit she thought she had conquered. On several of those times she had charged into the waiting room and quickly noted that the doctor was not visibly pacing the floor waiting for her. She had then in quick little movements settled herself on the sofa, opened a magazine, and tried to appear as if she had been patiently sitting there reading for at least ten minutes while *she* waited for *him*. While she would like to try such tactics today, she had long since learned that Dr. Odell had never been deceived, and had once even half teasingly accused her of enjoying the idea that she was waiting for him rather than he for her.

The next best thing to pretending punctuality

would be to go in through the open door before he came out to get her. Somehow it gave her the illusion of being more timely than he. Perhaps she could even catch him making a telephone call on her time! Momentarily she wondered why her mind was behaving as if she didn't know the man at all.

Dr. Odell had barely had time to heave himself out of his comfortable chair when he heard his outer door click and Helen came bustling into his office, closing the door behind her before he could do it himself. He was relieved and happy to see her, although a little puzzled by her sudden lapse into her former hyperactivity.

Before he could open his mouth to greet her, she began her barrage of excuses. "I'm sorry I'm late today," she began breathlessly, not sounding the least bit sorry. "Of all days in the world that I wanted to talk to you, it's today. I honestly think the gods had a summit meeting to keep me from getting here. The telephone—traffic was indescribable—and when I parked in the lot outside there was a funny noise in my car. I probably won't even be able to get home—do you think you might wait until I get my car started before you leave tonight—you don't have any more patients today, do you?" She paused for breath.

"Hello," the doctor said, smiling quietly. Helen smiled in return and said, "Hello, yourself." Her voice had come down about two octaves, and she added, "I was flying a bit high there, wasn't I?" She settled herself into the chair at the end of the couch opposite Dr. Odell's chair.

"You're a lot easier to bring down than you used to be." He didn't ask her why she was late, although he was curious, but he waited for her to tell him in her own inimitable manner. And she did.

"Actually all those excuses about the phone and traffic aren't quite accurate. They weren't any worse today than they are every day. The truth is I forgot about my appointment today." She waited a moment to gauge his response. "I don't know if I would have remembered it at all if Tom hadn't reminded me it was Thursday." (Okay you bastard. Now pass judgment on me, a poor sinner.)

"I really am surprised," the doctor said. "I suppose I should feel rejected, but I'm too curious to find out what brought on this monumental happening. You used to be late often, but you have never before forgotten your appointment." He would never really become accustomed to the short skirts, and he found it difficult to keep his eyes from her legs as she squirmed into a comfortable position in her chair.

"You're no more curious than I am," Helen answered. "I haven't even had time to think about it. Ever since Tom reminded me that I was supposed to be here, my energy has been spent in trying to get here. Maybe that's why traffic seemed worse and everything seemed to plot against my arrival." She thought for a moment before she continued, "You know, that's not exactly true either, what I just said. I could probably get by without telling you this, but I am wondering about it. Even after I knew I was late and broke speed records in getting over here, I then sat in the car for a full minute listening to a thud in my car. Then I took time to go clear down to the end of the hall to use the rest room and combed my hair and put on lipstick as usual. It was as if everything in me was telling me to hurry and get here, but my motor wouldn't respond to the accelerator."

"Okay," Dr. Odell said, after waiting for her to continue. "If you want me to say it instead of you, I'll say it. I'll be the therapist if you insist."

Helen giggled at this remark. "No, Teacher, I'll do my own dirty work." She assumed a pompous, pseudodignified pose and sat up straight in the chair, her dimples betraying her enjoyment: "Quote, Mrs. James, you have two sets of feelings simultaneously. One set of feelings tells you to do one thing; the other set tells you to do another. This, my dear lady, is called ambivalence." She relaxed back into her chair and tucked her legs under her.

"Come on, now, I was never that bad, was I?" Dr. Odell answered, smiling in reluctant appreciation of her mimicking him. He was aware that it was all too easy for him to become intellectualized and lecturing. His colleagues in the countertransference group had pointed out with annoying persistency this same characteristic. However, he realized that Helen would much prefer to discuss what she considered his shortcomings rather than uncover her own hidden feelings that led to her forgetting today's appointment.

"Of course," she added, "you said that in those days when you were being stuffy and formal before I loosened you up."

"Back to your mystery," he said, "even though it obviously is not your most preferred topic of conversation."

Helen was still reluctant to give up the bantering. She truly enjoyed her time with Dr. Odell, and she particularly liked to verbally spar with him about inconsequential matters. She was aware that this was a form of defensiveness and avoiding the issue, but today she was prolonging what Dr. Odell used to refer to as her "tea parties." (What is it that I am avoiding? My mind has gone blank. I can't even remember what it was that I was so eager to talk to him about.)

"I really don't consider it a mystery at all," she told him. "I mean after all—so I forgot my appointment. I'm sure I'm not the first patient you ever had who did that, am I? After all, I've been coming here twice a week for two years regularly as the mailman, and so I forget this one time. You're making a federal case out of it. Maybe I do have a little 'ambivalence.' For sixty dollars a week, I'm entitled to it."

She's going to play a hard game today, Dr. Odell thought. He leaned back in his chair and put his hands behind his head. Aloud he said to her, "I can see it all now. At the end of the hour"—he looked at his watch —"which is in thirty-two minutes, you will, as you leave, casually mention that you killed your grandfather this week, divorced your husband, abandoned your two children, and burned down your house since you saw me last, and you will wonder where all the time went that you couldn't seem to get around to telling me these things."

Helen smiled at his remarks, but they had struck a familiar note and she recognized the well-known beginnings of panic that she had felt so often in here. How many hours had she lain in mute agony on that couch with painful feelings overflowing inside her and responded with utter silence to Dr. Odell's gentle verbal prodding. It seemed sometimes that the more insistent and intense her feelings were, the more difficult it became to express them. She knew that these circumstances were more likely to occur at times when she most needed help and that her mental writhing increased with each passing minute.

She could imagine the clock ticking away louder and louder as if it were ticking away her life, but each time she would open her mouth to pour out her pain and discomfort and distress and fears, she felt as if an invisible hand were clamped over her mouth. On these occasions she could feel perspiration running down her sides under her dress. She worried that he could see the damp stains under her arms and would press her arms tightly to her body to conceal them. Then her hands would become clammy and tears inevitably would follow.

Only when Dr. Odell announced that the hour was over and she sat up to dry her eyes and gather her belongings together could she express whatever event or feeling had enveloped her. Thus it was during the last thirty seconds of various hours that she had told him the most important truths and feelings about herself. It was never that she consciously withheld these facts from him. It was more as if she could reveal her need for him only at a time when she knew further discussion could not follow.

Dr. Odell had watched Helen's face change during her thoughts. Gently he said, "Why don't you say it out loud? Will it help for me to say it for you? 'You can't help me. I don't need you. You don't like me.' If that's the sort of thing that's blocking you, don't let it be such a big deal."

Instead of being comforting, Dr. Odell's attempts to help her verbalize her feelings served to increase Helen's anxiety. She looked longingly at the couch for a moment and wished she were lying on it again as she had for many months. (At least I could avoid those probing eyes when I used to lie there staring at the ceiling.)

She stole a quick glance at the doctor. (Why should I feel so threatened? He looks the same as he always does, and his presence is usually comforting and even fun.)

She furtively studied him from the corner of her eye. Dr. Odell was of average height and had retained his muscular and athletic build, although there was the suggestion of a beginning paunch, one of the hazards of his profession. He was tanned and looked disgustingly healthy—probably from his regular Saturdays on the golf links. His face bore the expression of a good-natured Irishman, and the only discernible lines were laugh lines around his mouth and eyes, leaving his high forehead as unwrinkled as that of an adolescent. His hair was sandy and straight, without a hint of gray, and his only concession to the modern trend in men's hair styling was that he had grown a rather magnificent set of sideburns. His eyes were blue, a pale blue that reminded Helen of her father's eyes, so in contrast to the black, snapping eyes of her mother. (He looks less like a therapist than anyone I know. No Jewish accent, no beard, none of the cartoon characteristics so often associated with therapists.)

Now those blue eyes were zeroed in on her awaiting a response, and she squirmed in uneasiness and glanced again at the couch.

'I don't remember that couch being so appealing to you a little while back," he said. "Look, equal partner, I don't know what's going on today, but it's about time we find out."

"Sometimes I think you use that 'equal partner' phrase with me just when you're certain you have the upper hand. But it's true that the couch does look inviting to me today. But that's only because I'm sitting in the chair. When I was on the couch, the chair looked more appealing. Greener grass and all that stuff."

Helen reflected for a moment on what she remembered as her "couch ordeal." She had been terrified of the couch when Dr. Odell had first moved her to it after a few months of therapy. She still remembered his method of getting her there: "Come on now, you can't be chicken all your life. You've talked about the couch and heard stories about it and wondered about it, and now I think it's a good time for you to try it. You've been coming long enough to know quite a bit about therapy and to know me, and yet it seems very easy for you to focus on almost anything in here but your own feelings. I honestly think it will help you to try it this way for a while."

She had edged up to the couch as if it had hidden fangs, and when she first lay down the only parts of her that touched it were the back of her head and her heels. She had seldom felt so nervous or uncomfortable. Somehow she had believed that terrible and forbidden sexual feelings would engulf her, but her only feeling was an overwhelming sensation of helplessness. She had begun to cry. The rest of the hour was spent wiping tears and blowing her nose.

She had declared at the end of the hour that Dr. Odell's motive in moving her to a horizontal position was to make her feel inferior and to graphically illustrate that she was just another lowly patient while he was the elite superior therapist. She had felt inexplicably frightened and vulnerable and had the mental image of holding her frail, helpless arms out to the doctor supplicatingly and begging aloud for his help. This fantasy had so threatened her that she had been unable to tell him anything about it until several sessions later.

Helen now smiled at the doctor. "Having thought it over for a bit, I have decided the couch doesn't look so good to me after all. I was just remembering the buckets of tears I used to shed before you promoted me back to my 'equal' relationship with you in a chair."

"I'm really quite puzzled today as to where to put you. It seems to me that when you're on the couch you feel without talking, and in the chair you talk without feeling."

Dr. Odell's thoughts had also returned to the first day he had put Helen on the couch some eighteen months ago. He had been thoroughly astonished at the depth of her reaction. He knew that this resourceful, clever, seemingly self-sufficient woman would be threatened, but had not anticipated the intensity of her emotions. She had become the opposite of the independent, efficient self she presented to herself and the world. She had lain on the couch in abject misery, choked up and unable to verbalize a single sentence.

Her sudden transformation from a verbal, assertive, sophisticated woman to an incoherent, distraught, forlorn child alarmed him. He wondered if he had been premature in placing her on the couch and had overestimated her strength. Here was a woman he knew and liked, and it was painful for him to see her suffer. Part of him would have liked to release her immediately from the couch and console her. However, greater than his compassion was his belief that she would survive and benefit if they could both tough it out.

Helen had stayed on the couch for three months, all the while experiencing the most painful, extraordinary, and baffling feelings of her life. While Dr. Odell had some understanding of her desperate dependent needs, the use of all his skills never diminished her discomfort. The experience had served to illuminate but not to resolve her extreme problem with trusting or depending upon another person. What had

been merely hinted at while she was in the chair became the central problem when she was on the couch.
He now more fully realized that she was a woman
who was agonizingly suspended exactly between
complete trust and total mistrust. Had she trusted him
less than she did, she could have lain on the couch
without the disquieting longings rising so disturb-
ingly to the surface and adjusted much as she had to
the chair. Had she trusted him more, she could have
gradually revealed to the therapist—and to herself—
the nature of the dark, nameless emotions that were
choking her.

It seemed unbelievable to both of them that the
mere changing to a supine position on the couch had
served to illustrate the core of the problem. The combination of her undiminished misery and her continued inability to express it convinced Dr. Odell that
they were at an impasse. At his first hint that she
return to the chair, she leaped at the chance. It was
only after she was back in the chair that she verbalized
that she could only talk to him if she felt like an
"equal partner." She claimed that the couch had been
no help at all and had wasted "three months of her
money." However, while Dr. Odell cringed a little at
this assessment, he knew he had information about
her he knew he would never have gained but for the
ordeal of the couch.

Dr. Odell pulled his thoughts back to the present
and realized that Helen looked preoccupied. "Which
of us is daydreaming most today?" he asked. "I confess I was diverted into mulling over your three

months on the couch." He laughed for a moment. "I am still trying to get your money's worth out of it somehow."

"Actually I was just remembering something completely unrelated to you or me or therapy—or anything at all really."

"That's the best kind," Dr. Odell answered. When a patient said "completely unrelated," he picked up his ears for material usually both relevant and interesting. He leaned back in his chair with much the feeling he had had as a little boy when his first grade teacher had announced she was going to read a story "for fun."

"It's just a small incident that happened about, oh, at least twelve years ago, when we lived in western Kansas. It was when I was working as a medical secretary for two general practitioners in a little farm town you probably never heard of."

"Come on, quit stalling. You've got my interest now. I've jumped at the bait," he answered, smiling.

"We had a patient who came in regularly, usually to bring his little three-year-old boy. The man's name was Oscar Sampson, and his little boy was Oscar, Jr. The man wasn't very bright and was almost a caricature of the farm-boy type with hayseed coming out his ears. This image was made all the worse because he had a lisp and he pronounced his name 'Othcar Thampthon.' I can remember all of us girls in the office giggling and good-naturedly ridiculing him among ourselves."

Unexpectedly tears came to Helen's eyes and she

found it difficult to continue. The doctor waited in silence as she gathered her thoughts.

"Mr. Sampson's little boy was one of those perfect, angelic looking children who could have posed for a painting of a cherub. He had curly, tousled blond hair and round apple cheeks and blue eyes that could swallow you up—with eyelashes about three feet long. We all tended to make a fuss over little Oscar—isn't that a terrible name to give such a beautiful child?"

"A rose is a rose is a rose," Dr. Odell answered. "You haven't mentioned Mrs. Sampson. Where was the mother all this time?"

"I'm sorry. I thought I told you. Mrs. Sampson had left her husband and run away with another man when little Oscar was an infant. Perhaps that's partly why we doted on him so much. None of us could understand or imagine how a mother could leave this little boy, although he certainly didn't lack for attention from his father. Mr. Sampson almost worshiped that child, and you could see the pride in his eyes when he would bring little Oscar in for his shots or checkups. And it was a mutual admiration society. Oscar looked up at his father as if he were the embodiment of everything good in the world. In fact, Mr. Sampson almost took on a different perspective when his small son looked at him."

Tears were now streaming down Helen's face. (Dammit! why the hell am I telling him this story that has nothing to do with me? And why am I crying about it after all these years! I haven't even thought about Kansas for ten years. Any minute Dr. Odell is going to accuse me of being "resistive" and talking about everything but my own feelings.)

As she looked at Dr. Odell, however, he seemed quite interested in what she was saying and nodded for her to go on. Wiping her eyes and feeling slightly ridiculous, she continued.

"One Saturday morning—all the farmers used to come in on Saturday morning and combine their weekly marketing and shopping with their doctor's appointments—one Saturday morning Mr. Sampson rushed into the office carrying little Oscar in his arms. He was crying, and unashamedly let the tears run down his face onto his shirt."

"Mr. Sampson or Oscar was crying?"

"Mr. Sampson. Because Oscar was unconscious. He just dangled limply in his father's arms. It scared me to death, and I ran for Dr. Merrill, who was the only one of the doctors in the office that day. Dr. Merrill came out and hustled Mr. Sampson and Oscar back into one of the examining rooms. The morning rushed on because we were very busy, and I never heard any more about it until Monday."

She stopped speaking for a moment, and her face looked as if she were in pain. Finally Dr. Odell gently prodded her into continuing. "What was wrong with the little boy?"

"On Monday morning when I came in Dr. Merrill told us that little Oscar had spinal meningitis. He was running a 106 degree temperature and was in a coma. They didn't think he'd live—and even if he did, they felt there would be considerable brain damage. It was so dreadful to think of that beautiful, adorable little boy becoming a vegetable and of his father who had already lost his wife and whose very world revolved around his small son."

Dr. Odell had decided that the little boy must have died in the hospital and that this memory was still disturbing Helen, but he waited for her to finish the story in her own time.

"He was in the hospital for about two weeks. During that time, one day Dr. Merrill asked me to go over to the hospital on an errand. It was such a small town and the hospital was only a block away, so I nearly always walked when I had something to do there for the doctors. This particular day I had to go to the pediatric ward, and as I walked down the hall I passed little Oscar's room. I glanced in and I shall never forget the scene as long as I live.

"Mr. Sampson had a rocking chair in the room and was holding little Oscar and rocking him with tears running down his cheeks. His eyes were red, he was unshaven, and he looked a hundred years old. I doubt he even saw me. He was rocking his little boy and singing nursery rhymes to his unhearing ears, for the child was still unconscious. As I walked by I heard, 'And when the wind blowth, the cradle will rock.' Somehow his lisp made the scene even more poignant. I cried all the way back to the office."

Dr. Odell was still waiting to hear that the child had died, for now Helen was actually sobbing. Yet she didn't go on with her story. Finally he asked, "What happened to Oscar?"

"Oh, he got well. Everyone said it was nothing short of a miracle. They had only let Mr. Sampson in to stay with him and allowed him to rock Oscar because they felt the child was dying anyway and it could do no more harm. His father never left that room from the time his son entered the hospital. And not only did Oscar get well, but there was no brain damage at all. I saw them often after that when Mr. Sampson would bring Oscar in. Needless to say, we never again joked about his lisp. When I left Kansas a year later, the boy was thriving, and he and his father were still living alone together on the farm."

The doctor had become caught up in the story, and it took him several seconds to refocus on Helen's reason for telling it.

"That wasn't the finish I was expecting. Your tears had me convinced I was in for an unhappy ending. In fact, you still look sad. A happy ending and an unhappy woman. How can that be?"

Dr. Odell was often tempted to resort to the stereotyped therapist's phrases at such times. "What were your feelings as you told that story? What are you thinking about right now?" These overused cliches made him feel as if he were playing the role of a therapist rather than being one. He had learned from past experience with Helen that they served to make her feel like a "patient" in her own worst interpretation of the word. The use of these phrases alone was enough to spark her resistance and banish any thoughts or feelings she might otherwise have expressed.

"I guess I can't stand happy endings," Helen answered, still wiping away tears and trying to smile. "I honestly don't know why that incident still affects me so much. While I worked in the medical office, I saw far worse tragedies and really unhappy endings that I can hardly remember now. Yet I can never think of that scene of Oscar's father rocking him in that chair and singing to him without having tears come to my eyes." Tears came to her eyes again.

"You just proved that," Dr. Odell said gently. "I half felt like crying myself."

"But big boy's don't cry, do they?" Helen said sarcastically, with some of her self-assurance returning. The sarcasm was aimed more at herself than the doctor. She never failed to berate herself at an open display of tears.

Dr. Odell momentarily felt weary. She's back on her well-traveled road again, he thought, but she still can't read the road signs. In a hundred ways over the past two years she had voiced this same theme: To cry is to be childlike. To be childlike is to be unacceptable. Therefore, to cry is unacceptable. For a moment he hated the parent-conditioning that resulted in Helen's being so exasperatingly stupid and blind in this one area. For a woman who was perceptive and intelligent in most ways, she seemed to take pride in abysmal obtuseness about trust and dependency. He couldn't even give her credit for bringing up the "irrelevant" story she had just told, because she obviously did not see the relevancy at all. You are a dumb bitch, he thought to himself. This thought relieved his exasperation with her enough to modify his reply.

"Damn it, Helen. You really do try my patience. We have to have a special acceptance ceremony every time you shed a tear. You just told me a very poignant story. It obviously touched you—and me. It made you cry. Now, instead of being ashamed of crying, explain to me why you did cry."

Helen looked astonished. "I felt so sorry for the father, of course," she answered. (What a stupid damned question!)

"Why?" the doctor asked. "His son got well with no bad after effects, you told me."

"Because he suffered such pain," Helen said. "He was such a pathetic character to begin with." (He's either being obtuse or he's trying to make me angry.)

"But you've told me about other pathetic people suffering pain that didn't make you cry. You couldn't even remember their names."

"Well, maybe it was for the little boy that I cried," Helen answered more thoughtfully. "He was so little to have had so much trouble—his mother leaving him and then being so sick, poor baby."

"Poor baby, huh? Do you think you'd like anything about being in his spot?" The doctor's face had assumed an air of total innocence as he asked this crucial question.

"You dirty son-of-a-bitch, you trapped me

again," Helen said. "You know I have this one little weakness and you keep harping on it. Okay, okay, so maybe I envy the kid a little. It might be worth getting sick to get all that attention—and love."

"You almost didn't get 'love' in."

"Well, it's the kind of love only a child could get."

"And only a sick, helpless child can get this special kind of love? And only from a naive, backwoodsy father with a speech defect?"

"Damn it, you're twisting my words. I tell you a simple little story that happened to touch me very much," Helen retorted angrily. "Now you're making fun of me and the story, and I feel ashamed for having mentioned it to you. I'd like to change the subject."

"I would like to change the subject, too," Dr. Odell admitted, "because I now feel helpless. For a moment you really felt and understood the emotional point of your story, but now you've backed so far away from it that I'm your enemy. I was *not* making fun of you. I'm not the enemy. I'm on your side."

"Sometimes it sure doesn't feel like it," Helen said, still angry. "You keep exhorting me to show my feelings, tell about my feelings, don't be afraid of my feelings. Then when I do these very things—and they make me cry—you come up with that nasty 'backwoodsy father' remark and make me feel ridiculous. All your attitude serves to do is make me feel like shutting my mouth about anything but the weather —and maybe even that."

"Well," the doctor answered, with a wry smile, "this is just the first time I have ever felt that I had to grow six inches, develop a lisp, and have hayseed in my hair before I could be considered trustworthy or capable of loving someone. Will you make an absolute promise to me that if I make these changes then . . . "

Helen's anger was overcome at this point by her sense of humor. "At least you're a clever and humorous enemy." His last silly remark had made her stop and think about what part of the story had brought on the feelings and the tears. (Do I really want to be a child? Dr. Odell seems to want me to admit it regularly twice a week. What would it be like to be totally cared for and loved? Just for myself.) She was momentarily able to envision herself being rocked and sung to and cherished, but the sensation was fleeting.

"Okay," she said. "Suppose you're right for the sake of argument. Let's say I would like to be a child. I would like to be taken care of and loved. What good would it do me to admit it? Would it mean that I can quit my job tomorrow and stay home and be a parasite? Can I suddenly toss my responsibilities to the wind and say, 'World, love and take care of me. I'm depending on you.' Suppose I would like to be a child again? I can't. So what good does wishing do me?"

"For one thing you wouldn't have to come in here twice a week and verbally punch me in the nose to prove how aggressively adult you are," Dr. Odell answered. He gave intense thought for a brief moment to the wording of a serious answer to her question. He knew they were at the very crux of her problem and he had the feeling that a great deal hinged on his response.

This was the closest she had ever come to linking her clinging, dependent emotions to her own yearnings. She cried easily in the movies and wept when reading touching passages in books and readily reported to him about having felt sad when watching maudlin television shows. She had set rules as to when to cry and when not to cry. Her rules declared that it was adult to feel sympathy and pity for the misfortunes of others but childish to feel them for herself. Her admission of wishing to be a child Dr. Odell felt to be a great stride. He felt as if he had puzzled too long as Helen opened her mouth and began to speak.

"Don't have an answer, do you?" she said smugly.

"You really are a rotten patient, you know," he said. "Here I am trying to think up a brilliant answer at a delicate moment, and you've made me lose my train of thought."

Whether he knew it or not, the doctor had just said the right words. Helen visibly relaxed. Any admission on his part of fallibility or fumbling for words endeared him to Helen. Although it had certainly been unplanned on his part, his very act of groping for the correct response had made him appear more human to her. It made her more comfortable about seeking out and admitting her own weaknesses.

"Go on, Great One. I do feel in a little more receptive frame of mind." She smiled and scooted her chair a little closer to him. Without either of them realizing it, she had communicated to him a fraction of an inch more trust in the last minute.

"I guess what I was so delicately trying to phrase was that I am proud of you for being so brave. I know it was both frightening and daring for you to even entertain the notion that you want a close relationship such as little Oscar and his father had."

Helen made a semblance of a curtsy in her chair. "I feel honored at your praise, kind sir. But you still haven't answered my question. Okay. I've admitted that sometimes I'd like to be a child. I'd love to be loved and taken care of and protected. But I am an adult with adult responsibilities. How can my admission possibly be so worthwhile?"

"Think about it for a moment. Don't you feel closer to me than you did before we discussed this incident about Oscar? Isn't it a relief to know that I, another human being, know your 'worst' secret—that you'd like to be a loved child — and think more of you rather than less?"

"That's all very fine between you and me. But what do you suppose my husband would do if I suddenly became a genuine clinging vine? How would my boss, Tom, respond if I broke into childish tears just because both phones were ringing at once and three irritating clients were waiting? What if I responded to my children's tantrums with a tantrum of my own? I have to admit the idea of this kind of behavior is sort of appealing, but let's face it, it's not very practical when you are living in the adult world."

(My God, he looks rational enough. He doesn't even seem to realize that I've just advanced a really crazy theory. Maybe he just isn't listening. He can't be proposing that I behave that way? Am I spending thirty dollars an hour to learn to act as a three-year-old already knows how? Obviously, I am not getting through to him. He doesn't understand my point. Maybe he's tired. I'll try again.)

"What I'm trying to say, my friend, and obviously not succeeding in getting across to you is this: Yes. I think it would be great to be a child and have somebody take care of me and feed me and tuck me in. So what? What good does admitting it do? And don't give me any more of that crap about my 'worst secret.' I think you just said that because now that I've admitted it, you don't have any answer for me."

"For starters," he replied, "you could possibly satisfy some of those childish longings. You certainly have overdemonstrated your adulthood and there's room for the child . . . "

"Oh, Jesus! You've got to be kidding! I wasn't even allowed to be a child when I was one. I was always told to be a big girl. 'Big girls don't do this, big girls don't do that, big girls don't cry.' What are you trying to do to me? I thought all this therapy bit was to help a person grow up—not regress. Isn't that your fancy doctor term for retreating back to childhood?

"Well, let me tell you about some of those childish longings you so blandly mentioned. When I was eight years old—no great age you will admit? A child, okay? When I was eight years old we lived in that crummy little house that would be condemned as unlivable in this poverty-conscious age. All three rooms were covered with cold linoleum. We had running water but that was about all. For heat we had one of those potbellied stoves that cooked you on one side while you froze on the other, so that you had to keep turning all the time. It had to be continually fed wood and coal. They look ever so charming in the colonial section in the house-and-garden magazines, but believe me, in those magazines they are for looks only and I'll bet the house is heated with central heating and that shiny black potbellied stove is strictly for effect.

"My parents both worked, as you already know. They both left in the morning before it was even light. One day I was home with a godawful sore throat—a chronic malady of my so-called childhood—and when I woke up that morning feeling as if I had swallowed slivers of glass, nobody was home. I realized that my mother had let me sleep late and that she and Daddy had gone on to work.

"Then I realized the room was ice cold. I mean so cold that I couldn't even let myself move under the blankets for fear of letting some of that cold air in. I had so many covers on me I could hardly turn over in the bed. I guess my folks had tried to bank the fire in the stove—is that the right word? Bank? Anyway the fire had gone out. Also I was hungry. I wondered how I could get that stove to put forth some heat, but it just sat mocking me. It was as cold as I was.

"I thought about getting up and making a peanut butter sandwich—the extent of my culinary talent even though I was such a 'big girl'——but the thought of taking those twelve or so steps on that linoleum to the kitchen made the hunger pangs bearable. I would have liked to cry, but 'big girls don't cry.' So I just lay there all morning trying not to move or to swallow very often and wondering if the day would ever pass or if I would spend the rest of my life alone, hungry, and cold.

"At about twelve-thirty there was a knock at the door. It scared me. Since I was home alone, I didn't know whether to be quiet and hope whoever it was would go away, or try to get up and go answer the door or just yell, 'Come in,' and hope it wasn't a burglar or a murderer or monster. I settled on the 'big girl' solution and called for whoever it was to come in.

"Our next door neighbor, Mrs. Barnes, came in all smiling and smelling of homemade bread. She had a tray with her on which was a huge mug of hot soup, some homemade bread wrapped in a napkin and still warm, and a bowl of gorgeous red jello. Nobody ever looked so motherly and adult to me before. She smiled and chatted and patted me on the head and muttered small comforts about my throat, all the while expertly building a roaring hot fire in that miserable stove. Then she left and said she'd be back in a little while to see how I was getting along and to pick up the dishes, and that she'd bring me a book or a magazine if I wanted one.

"Now, wouldn't you think I would feel better

after all that nice mothering? Well, I didn't. After Mrs. Barnes left, I cried for the first time that day. The tears I had held back so bravely all morning just gushed. I lay in bed in that nice, warm, snug room with my tummy full of hot soup and cried all afternoon. I simply wallowed in self-pity. How I pitied that poor little girl I had been that morning, cold, alone, hungry, with no one to take care of her, deserted by mother and father, and left to die of hunger and exposure! How could anyone treat a child like that!

"Don't you see? I could cry only after an adult had treated me as if I were a child. Only then could I really believe I was a child. I had a perfectly lovely afternoon, reflecting on my earlier misery in comfort. I think I even enjoyed the standard childhood fantasy that I had been abandoned on my parents' doorstep and was really an orphan—princess, yet. How would my real parents, the King and Queen, feel if they knew how their little darling had been treated? This would bring on lovely, fresh gushes of tears. But only when I was alone. I was still a 'big girl' and I didn't want anyone to see me crying."

Dr. Odell had been listening carefully. "Be careful now, or you might answer your own question," he said. "Remember a little while ago you did challenge me to give you some good reasons for admitting to even the existence of the child part of yourself. Notice your own comparison in the story you just told me about yourself. Weren't you much happier during the afternoon when you were feeling like a protected child than you were in the morning being a 'big girl'? Even though you cried?"

"I just connected it with something entirely different. Eureka! Listen to this, old know-it-all. Is it just possible that I was comparing sick little Oscar with sick little Helen? And also comparing the kind of treatment they got? Because that feels right to me. I think what I most wanted that morning when I was sick and cold and hungry was a parent just like 'Mr. Thampton' to rock and hold me and sing to me. Do you suppose—just—possibly—that is why the story has stuck in my head for so long?" (I suppose I should feel ridiculous confessing such an idea, but somehow I don't. My God. Next I'll be sucking my thumb or bringing a pacifier to therapy with me.)

Dr. Odell actually applauded. "Brilliant," he said with praise in his voice. "I feel sure you're right, and you did beat me to the draw."

"Whee!" Helen said. "A new first!"

"I do feel a little chagrined that you saw the linkage between these two stories before I did. I admit I was sitting here thinking you wore permanent blinders in regard to your dependent feelings. But congratulations! You just took a giant step toward being really independent."

Chapter 4

The significance of Helen's insight impressed Dr. Odell as he compared her current self-understanding with her closed mind and defensive behavior when he had first met her.

Helen's initial feelings that she needed help had not come gradually and built up. They had hit her suddenly and unexpectedly. She could remember the exact date, the day of the week, and almost the minute when she had become engulfed and overwhelmed with a sense of fear and dread. She later described the episode to Dr. Odell as feeling that her sanity had suddenly been cut from its moorings and that she was hopelessly drifting away from solid ground.

It was a Wednesday two years ago. She was tired when she got up that morning. Even after she had showered and dressed for the office, the disheveled, unmade bed still held appeal for her. She considered calling her boss, Tom, and telling him she was sick. However, she had the illogical conviction that if she did this, she would truly become ill in punishment for her lie.

She haphazardly made the bed and went to the kitchen for coffee. Her two children were at summer camp, and Steve had got up and left early for his office. She was glad he wasn't there. Without the children as buffers, they had had a loud argument the night before. It was the same argument they had periodically, usually on pay day, each attacking the other for spending money needlessly when there was never enough to go around. They alternately accused each other of extravagance or stinginess, depending upon who had bought what.

She had their script memorized and knew every line that was to follow when he opened their Goldwater's charge account bill and spotted the ticket for three pairs of Andrew Geller shoes.

"Is this charge ticket right? You bought three pairs of shoes?" All innocence in his tone.

"Yes, it's right." Equal innocence.

"They surely made a mistake on the price. One hundred and two dollars and ninety-six cents for three pair of shoes?" Is that sarcasm or disbelief in his voice?

"They made no mistake. Thirty-three dollars times three equals ninety-nine dollars plus tax. Incidentally, they were thirty-three dollars on sale." Now she knew they were girding for battle. She wished she had hidden those damned shoes under the bed and brought them out one pair at a time. She knew her real mistake was not getting to the bill before Steve did. It usually made no difference, because he almost never looked at the bills anyway but merely handed them to her to pay. She began to wonder what his motive was in so carefully checking each ticket.

"On sale," he said. "Now I know where the 'gold' in Goldwater's came from. Did it occur to you that you wouldn't wear your shoes out so fast if you didn't spend so much time chasing up and down the aisles of department stores?" The gauntlet was thrown. She knew what they were sliding into, but she was powerless as always to stop it.

"Oh, is that right? Well, my fine wonderful, providing husband, how is it that I manage to bring home $800 a month if I am spending so much time in department stores? If I want to spend one eighth—*one eighth*—of my money on myself, I believe I am entitled. I think I contribute more than my share around here and it's my privilege to spend some of it as I like."

"But you spend that one eighth four times each month. And the rest of it goes for babysitters, car expenses, lunches, and taxes. So don't give me that 'contributing more than my share' bit. You know damned well you work because you'd rather be in an office than home doing housework."

"Doing housework!" she said. "Well, who the hell do you think does the housework around here? Do you think the fairy godmother slips in quietly each day and waves her hand so that the dishes are done and the beds made and dinner ready each night when you get home? By God, I do as much housework as any other housewife—and more than a lot of them who spend their time watching soap operas, drinking coffee, and gossiping. Is that the kind of wife you're longing for? Because if it is, get a $10,000 a year raise and I can afford to do it."

"No, I definitely think that any woman with three brand new pairs of Andrew Geller shoes shouldn't wear them around the house to dust in but should wear them to a fancy office," he said caustically.

"Why is it that you are suddenly taking such an interest in our finances anyway?" she asked. "You know damned well that for fifteen years I have written every check for this household, balanced all the bank statements, and have been delegated most of the worrying. Then about once a year you like to put on this big show of the responsible, capable man in complete command of all the household affairs. Well, you don't kid me, Steve. Most of the time you don't have the faintest notion of how much money we have, how much we owe, or to whom we owe it. So you can cut the performance if it is for my benefit. If you really want to be a big man, take the damned bills and handle the checking account yourself. Then once a year I will come to you and complain about the way you do it."

"I notice that while you are demanding credit for handling things so beautifully you haven't saved one dime for these fifteen years—no savings, no investments, nothing to fall back on if we should have a real emergency."

"So now that's my job, too! Handling all the investments? First you want a housewife and now you want an investment broker. You're supposed to be the man in the family. Why don't you make some investments to care for us in our old age—which seems frighteningly close to me tonight?" Her frustration in unsuccessfully trying to get credit for achievement in any area of her life was turning her rage into feelings of hurt, and she could feel stinging tears begin to well up in her eyes, followed by familiar feelings of defenselessness.

"All right, I will," he said. "I want to take over the investments. If you think you can turn over the reins to me. You know you love to control that damned checkbook, so I doubt if you can stand to let me make a decision about an investment anyway. You never have."

"Never let you!" she said. Now the tears were flowing uncontrolled. "How can you say that? You have never even brought the subject up for discussion before this minute. You haven't even looked at the checkbook for six months."

"I never can find the damned thing. Just tell me straight out—how much money do we have in the bank?"

"Enough to pay these bills you see before you and about $200 left over."

"Fine. Give me a check for the $200. I have an investment in mind."

"What kind of an investment?" Helen asked warily. She knew now that she had been set up and she waited for the blow to fall.

"See? That's just what I mean. I can't even get $200 back out of my $1500 check without getting the third degree and telling you where every cent of it is

going to. That's just what we've been talking about."
He spread his arms in a what's-the-use gesture.

Now she was trapped. Either she gave him the
$200 unquestioningly or she withheld it and proved
that she was controlling and stingy and all the other
adjectives he had applied to her. She started to make
out the check when it suddenly occurred to her that
she might be giving quiet permission for some "investment" that might be more far-reaching than Steve had
implied. They seldom had even $200 left at the end
of the month. Did his investment plans go beyond
this $200? She hesitated and then laid the pen down.

"You write the check. Your hands aren't painted
on."

Steve leaped up from the kitchen table where
they were sitting with the bills spread out before
them. "Forget it, damn it! Forget the whole thing!
This is just what I might have expected of you. If I
have to go through this kind of scene every month
just to protect our future, it just isn't worth it."

"Every month? What makes you think we will
have $200 extra every month?"

"You surely don't think one $200 check is going
to provide any kind of protection against future disaster, do you?" he retorted, assuming his look of male
authority. "I'll tell you what I had in mind. I have a
chance to buy half interest in a used airplane with
Harry Simms at the office. It sure wouldn't hurt my
position when he takes in the next partner. We can
get into this deal with a couple of hundred dollars
apiece — a month — the plane only costs $9,000 with

its major, and the profits to me and the company could be limitless."

Helen was speechless. An airplane! An airplane? As an investment? Nine thousand dollars? The only question she could form was, "What's a major?"

"A major overhaul, completely checked out, like new," he answered, his tone implying condescension. Now his approach had changed completely. Where there had been baiting and sarcasm, there was now enthusiasm and persuasiveness. "We think we can talk the Chairman of the Board into using the plane for making deliveries of refrigeration parts all over the state. Think what that would do to our competition. Besides we could use the plane ourselves on weekends for the family—maybe fly down to Mexico or over to the coast."

Helen's mind was beginning to clear. "Two hundred dollars a month each? But you don't even know how to fly! What kind of a plane?" she asked.

He brushed off her questions as he would an aggravating fly. "Well, of course I would have to take some flying lessons," he said. "And the plane is a real little beauty. It's a 150 Cessna."

Helen's boss, Tom, owned an airplane. Her numbed brain began to flash figures at her. She remembered writing sizable checks for prohibitive insurance premiums, tiedown space, and required FAA maintenance overhauls. She had also written the checks for Tom's flying lessons, $500 to get his private pilot's license and another $500 for instrument rating. Tom, a successful attorney whose income tripled hers and Steven's together, often complained bitterly that he didn't know how much longer he could afford to keep his plane.

She opened her mouth to speak, but she had so much to say she didn't know where to start. Finally she said, "I'll take the shoes back."

Steve threw his arms into the air then dropped them to his sides in mock resignation. "Typical Helen behavior." This phrase was his standard ending of an argument when he knew he had lost. "I should have known when I started that you wouldn't even listen. Forget I ever mentioned it."

"But, Steven," she said, trying to assume a reasonable attitude, "remember all the expenses and trouble Tom has had with his plane? Doesn't he have a Cessna 150, too? And doesn't it only hold two people?"

He glared at her with real contempt. "It has a jump seat," he said. "For $9000 maybe you'd like me to find you a nice, slightly used 747." He started toward the front door.

"But Steve . . . " she began.

"Forget it! You win, you win! I give up. I'm going over to the Skull n' Crossbones where people are more friendly." The door slammed behind him.

Helen slumped in her chair. Here she is folks, the big $200 winner, she thought bitterly to herself as she wiped away tears that were running down her chin. How come every time I am pronounced the winner, I feel like such a damned stupid loser. She began sorting the bills and automatically writing checks.

Her attention span was at an all-time low, and her mind was swept from her accounting duties by alternating waves of anger and self-pity.

"Why can't I ever be the loser?" she said to herself. The thought of Steve sitting happily in his favorite bar, probably surrounded by several buddies and cocktail waitresses waving their nearly bare behinds at him brought further tears of anger which felt like acid being squeezed from her eyes. I wonder if I could have the locks on the house changed before he gets back, she wondered idly. Maybe he'll get so drunk he'll get himself killed on the way home. This thought was momentarily so satisfying and then so guilt producing, she went back to her check writing to punish herself and dispel the image.

The unending, never-changing arguments about money usually left Helen angry and sleepless. That night, however, she felt drained of any emotion now that the last accusation had been flung and the last check written. She simply felt exhausted and wanted to be left in peace. She turned off the kitchen light and hurriedly prepared for bed. As she put her head on the pillow, she hoped she would sleep immediately. She was afraid that if she were still awake when Steve returned home, he might take up where he had left off.

Helen poured herself a second cup of coffee and wondered why she always played these painful scenes back to herself the next day. She never relived happy or successful experiences over and over in this way. Nor did she seem to learn anything that prevented or altered the next struggle with Steve.

Whereas most people after a night's sleep and in the clear light of day are able to view events of the previous evening with more clarity, the reverse was true of Helen. During the battle she had felt Steve was being unreasonable, extravagant, and accusatory. This morning she wasn't sure but that the fault was entirely hers. Part of what he said was certainly true. She was the one who had kept the budget and paid the bills all their married lives. It was surely true that they had no investments and savings. She undeniably had bought three pair of shoes. He had the knack of making her feel if she had handled their affairs more capably, they now could afford a 747. It somehow seemed vastly unfair to her though that she should now feel that the shoes would be the cause of their spending their old age on the County Farm—or wherever they sent penniless old people with no foresight.

Damn it, the bills did bother her. She never bought anything for herself until all their obligations had been met. She did make a lot of money "for a woman," she thought, and she felt that if she were willing to work full time and take care of the house with no help, there had to be some icing on the cake to make it worthwhile. The trouble was the icing always seemed to make her sick.

She knew she could turn the checkbook over to Steve. The thought unnerved her, because she knew that if she did, the airplane and flying lessons would take precedence over the bills, and she would no longer have any control over her own purchases. It was an experience similar to this early in their marriage that had resulted in her taking over the budget in the first place so long ago—the result of which had left them the only newlyweds she knew who had owned an outboard motor boat but no furniture.

Pushing the thoughts of her past and present marital problems to the back of her mind, Helen gathered up her purse and a file folder she had brought home from the office. She locked the front door behind her, went outside, and opened the garage door. There stood her 1965 Ford, dirty and neglected. The dent in the rear fender that she had ignored for three years now jarred her and seemed to mock her own mood. I feel dented, too, she thought. She climbed into the front seat, inserted the key in the ignition and turned it. There was not a sound, not even a promising grind. With that fatal knowledge that all automobile owners have about their own cars, she knew it was not going to start; nevertheless, she tried again— and again. Perspiration was beginning to run down her sides and her forehead was damp. On this August morning in Phoenix, the temperature was already ninety-five degrees at eight forty-five. Frustration combined with the heat to make her feel prickly all over, and she had the sudden impulse to rip off her wig and her girdle and stand in the driveway and scream.

After what seemed an interminable interval of thwarted attempts and frustrations, waiting for the service station truck to arrive and put a quick charge on her battery, she arrived at her office damp, wrinkled, hot, mad—and forty minutes late. The situation would have been intolerable except she had the uneasy sensation that none of this was really happening to her. She felt more like an uninvolved observer watching an unfortunate, idiotic woman going through the paces of a pointless endurance test. Thus she settled herself at her desk with a deceiving calm that belied her true state.

Ordinarily she would have dramatically described the morning to Tom, exaggerating the episode just enough to amuse him, and it would have ended with his taking her to the first floor coffee shop and their laughing the incident into its proper perspective. This morning, however, she made only the vaguest reference to the reason for her tardiness, sat down at her desk, and began immediately to shuffle papers and feign involvement in her work. Tom's puzzled expression went unnoticed by her.

While Helen appeared to be absorbed in proofreading a legal brief she had typed the day before, her attention was far removed from it. Her mind had returned to the conflict with Steve the night before and her difficulties with her aging car this morning. (My marriage and my car are disintegrating simultaneously. I wonder which will totally fall apart first?) She had the hysterical thought that maybe if she agreed to Steve's buying the airplane, he might let her fly it to the office each day.

She tried to shake these irrational thoughts from her head and made a real effort to concentrate on the brief, but her brain behaved as if it weren't receiving the correct signals. She reread the first paragraph three times and still didn't know what it said. She marveled at the efficiency of the person she had been yesterday who had been able to type these complicated, intellectual phrases when today she couldn't even comprehend their meaning.

(What is happening to me? I feel like a machine that is whirling madly and out of control but is not in gear. I must stop and think it through. If I just start from the beginning, surely I will understand what is wrong with me. It can't be simply the fight with Steven—heaven knows if it were that, I would have had to be locked up long ago. Besides I didn't feel this way after the fight last night. I can't believe that my car's not starting this morning could derange me. Yet it was the car incident that seemed to start me on these revolving, senseless thoughts.)

She was startled by Tom's sudden appearance at her desk. He looked at her quizzically. "Going to coffee this morning?" he asked her.

She couldn't bring herself to look up at him for fear all the tumbling, irrational thoughts in her head might show through her eyes. She kept her gaze on the brief as she answered, "No, Tom, not this morning. I don't feel I'd be very good company today."

She was aware of Tom's hesitancy before he started out the door. It was the first morning in months that they had not had coffee together, and she could not explain to him that she didn't think she would hold together long enough to get to the coffee shop. She felt guilty though, because Tom looked puzzled and uncertain. She managed a weak smile and called after him, "I'd thought I'd impress my boss by making up some of the time I was late this morning." Tom smiled, seemed to accept her excuse, and went on without her.

As soon as she was left alone in the office, she wished she had gone with him, but she couldn't bring herself to inflict her presence on anyone this morning. She didn't know what sort of behavior she could expect from herself. The feelings of foreboding and dread she was experiencing were alien to her. Fragments of thoughts rushed at her so quickly she could not hang on to any one of them long enough to decipher it. She considered talking to Tom about the strangeness she was feeling today. (But how would I describe it without sounding like an overdramatic fool? I can't believe the way I feel myself. How could I make Tom understand? He'd only pat me on the shoulder and tell me I've been working too hard—or I am just "being female"—and I don't think I could take that kind of treatment right now.)

She suddenly felt afraid of being alone. She had a sense of alienation. This office where she had spent forty hours a week for the last four years seemed peculiar and unreal. The room appeared smaller to her, and the objects and furniture with which she was so familiar looked strangely remote yet sharply defined, as if a camera which had been out of focus had suddenly been overcorrected. She opened and closed her eyes and looked again, trying to shake off the distorted image. Her hands were cold and wet and she rubbed them together. Her head ached, and each beat of her heart felt as though it were pumping inside her head.

She tried to think. It was like being on a runaway horse and losing the reins. She knew she had to do something—anything—which would return the world to normal. Where had it started? Her husband? The car? Back to the beginning. (But I've been back to the beginning before and it's like playing the same record over and over on the phonograph and reaching the same ending each time.) The repetitive thoughts went round and round in her head until she felt that they had worn a groove that was permanent. In the groove whirled images of new shoes, cars, and airplanes, and each time she thought of them the groove wore deeper.

With an effort she arose from her desk and went to the window. Tom's office was on the ninth floor of the building, and she stared down at the traffic on North Central Avenue. Miraculously she could feel normalcy returning and relief flooded her. She turned and looked back at the office again. The unreal feelings had fled as quickly as they had come. She felt grateful as one does after a narrow escape from danger.

With the relief came clarity of mind so that she was able to reflect on the frightening and bewildering experience. She looked at her watch and realized Tom had been gone for only ten minutes; yet the interval of her "spell" had seemed an eternity. (When might it strike again? I can't live through an attack like that again. That must be how crazy people feel.) This was the first time she had allowed herself to think about the word "crazy." (There must be something I can do to prevent that kind of out-of-control helplessness returning. I can't do anything about Steve—if my fight with him provoked the feelings. But by God, I certainly can and will do something about my car.)

To Helen it was as if some mysterious force had caused her anxiety and some equally mysterious and magical force had banished it, and her practical mind could relate these two events to nothing but her car. Since it was the car that was at fault, the thing to do was get rid of the car. Her mind had made the connection in one leap.

(Maybe my car's not starting this morning was a warning. Possibly all these frightening thoughts are a premonition. Never having had a premonition before, how do I know if this isn't what they are like? Next time the brakes might fail and I'll be killed.) She even began to think that this morning's episode was a lucky occurrence.

(I need a new car anyway. If I don't use the money to buy a car, Steve will use it to buy an airplane or for some other crazy scheme. Why should I drive an eight-year-old clunker with a dented fender when he is provided with a new company car every two years? He'd feel disgraced if he had to drive my car for a week.) Her decision was made. She would go out and look at cars on her lunch hour.

The remainder of her morning was spent in efficient and industrious activity, wherein she actually did complete as much work as she routinely did every morning. Her attack of anxiety was definitely a thing of the past, only vaguely remembered.

At one fifteen she eased her "new" two-year-old Lincoln Continental into the parking lot at her office. She was sure no one could tell it wasn't right out of the factory because the new ones hadn't changed body styles. The car had only 15,000 miles on it, but reflected a savings of half over its original price. Helen did not dwell on the difference in price between her old 1965 Ford and the Lincoln—only the difference between the two-year-old Lincoln and a new Lincoln. She rarely thought as much about what she spent as how much she had saved. She had not gone out with the intent of buying a luxury automobile, but when she discovered she could have the Lincoln for the same amount as a brand new Chevy, there was no contest.

She pulled the car into her parking place and sat for a moment listening to the purr of its engine. She rolled all the electric windows down and back up again as the air conditioning blew on her at a comfortable seventy-two degrees. She adjusted the seat upward a bit, then forward a trifle, and set a pushbutton on the stereo radio at her favorite FM station. She felt so exhilarated she giggled aloud. (It is gorgeous. It's the most beautiful, magnificent thing I have ever seen.) She patted the leather seat affectionately, and was hesitant to leave it for her office.

By two forty-five she had brought Tom and half the secretaries from her floor down to see the car. Their oohs and ahs had stimulated her excitement,

and the few envious glances had made her feel privi-
leged indeed. She sailed through the remainder of the
afternoon in grand style, in a state of new euphoria,
complimenting herself on how well she had solved her
problem.

Her state of well-being lasted until she got into
her new car to go home. As she turned the key in the
ignition, she thought clearly for the first time about
the papers in the glove compartment that Steve would
have to cosign with her for the loan on the car. All
the terrifying, engulfing feelings of panic that she
had experienced in the morning returned in triple
intensity. The first shock wave was the anxiety itself;
the second was the horror that it had returned. The
third paralyzing impact was that the panic now
seemed totally unrelated to the car.

She felt dimly aware that it would be wise to sit
for a moment and wait for these dangerous feelings
to ebb before she drove out of the office garage. But
the urgent need to do something—anything—to push
the feelings away overcame any thought of caution
or delay. She roared out of the garage, totally oblivious
to the smile and wave of the parking lot attendant
whose greeting she had always returned in the past.

She felt feverish and flushed, and her heart was
beating hard and fast. It was more as if she had many
hearts, one at each pulse point, and each was beating
its own exclusive and competitive rhythm. Her throat
was dry. She had the fleeting, vague idea that she
should pull over to the side of the road, but the car
seemed to be driving itself. Traffic sounds penetrated

her ears but were rendered meaningless when they reached her brain. She moved automatically with the stream of traffic, her eyes fixed and unseeing except for the car ahead of her. She felt that the passage of time was her only promise of release, for surely she could not remain suspended in this state of numb terror. But time played tricks on her, holding her mind in an iron vise of panic while allowing her body to move through it. Time became an enemy rather than an ally.

Because of her state of mind, she was surprised when she realized she was in front of her own house. As she pulled into the driveway, she grasped at the straw of an idea that once inside her familiar walls she would feel normal again. She parked the car in the garage and ran to the front door. Her legs felt as if they were made of jello.

She stood inside the front door and waited for the familiarity of her house to magically restore her. It didn't work.

She felt much the same as she had once when she had got lost on the way to the bathroom in the middle of the night. She hadn't turned on the lights and in her sleepy state she had felt along the wall for the bathroom door but had misjudged where she was and opened the closet door by mistake. She had walked into the closet and became entangled in winter coats. She had become so totally disoriented she could not find the light switch, the door, or any other object for a point of reference. It took her several minutes of confused fumbling and groping to find her way out of her own hall closet. She had felt frightened and lost. She

knew where everything was supposed to be but nothing seemed to be where it should be and she wondered if she had awakened in a strange place. Her
relief at finding the bathroom light switch had been
immense. Such relief was not now forthcoming.

(What a ridiculous comparison. It's not the middle of the night or dark and I am not lost. I actually
feel afraid. Almost as if the devil had chased me home
and is outside the door waiting to follow me in. My
God! I must be going crazy. I'm losing my mind.)

This was the first time in her life that Helen had
actually entertained the idea that there was something wrong inside her head. Many times in the past
she had shouted at her children, "You're going to
drive me crazy if you don't wipe your feet," or "Turn
that TV down before I lose my mind." Her thoughts
now, as she stood weak-kneed and bewildered and
alone inside her front door were far removed from
those other occasions.

As she changed from her office attire into an old
pair of shorts and shirt, she turned this new idea
around in her mind. She contemplated it with a
strange calmness. The urge to "do something" vanished. She had gained a slight element of control in
being able to name what she later referred to as her
"scares" to Dr. Odell. She felt she had nothing to do
now but contain her newly discovered lunacy until
she could outwrestle it. She marveled at her sudden
gain in strength and power because she had put a
name to what she was fighting. She was fighting her
own personal loneliness. Her "scares." She wished

momentarily that the children were home from camp to distract her from herself, and then immediately was glad they were still gone so they couldn't see her until she had vanquished this formless demon inside her head.

By the time Steve walked in the door Helen had dinner on the table.

"Who's here in the Lincoln Continental?" he asked, preferring to ignore their last hostile words.

Those were the last spoken words Helen clearly remembered that evening as she lay sleepless with Steve snoring beside her. She hated him for his ability to immediately fall asleep after every fight—or anything else. Bits and fragments came back to her but they became so entangled in arguments from the past, she didn't try to separate them into what had happened tonight. Steve's phrases about "ruinous extravagance" and "impulsive selfishness" and "impending bankruptcy" floated through her mind, along with her own defensive countercharges of his being "uncaring about her safety in that old car," and "being jealous that she might catch up with him in his fancy company car." He had given in easier than she thought he would and signed the papers for the bank loan, looking resigned and martyred, and ending the episode by stating to her that the car was hers, the payments were hers, and he never wanted to have anything further to do with it.

As she lay in bed now, her dry eyes beyond tears, she wondered if this would be the most expensive "win" she had ever had. She guessed his true reason for acquiescing so easily was that he now had the upper hand. Anything he did now, even buying a 747, would be justifiable.

When she finally slept around three o'clock in the morning, she dreamed of being pursued by a huge, gleaming automobile out of which someone unseen was tossing one hundred dollar bills. As the car bore down on her, she saw that the grille was actually the jaws of a shark. She escaped it only by running into a dense, heavy bank of fog in which she became irretrievably lost.

The tone of this dream formed the background for the next two months of Helen's life. She felt as if she were in a slow, spiraling descent into a black abyss. She tried to cope with the "scares" with various impotent actions. She made hesitant but repeated attempts to try to discuss her increasing sense of terror with Steve. He was at first astonished and then he became sympathetic, much as he would be if she had a virus. When his sympathy failed to "bring her out of it," he became impatient and even bored. He finally got angry and demanded that she "shape up and assume her responsibilities." This last remark was directed at her when she let him run out of clean underwear for the first time in their married life.

Steven's complaints had some merit, for she had become unable to cope with her duties both at home and at the office, and had let her household responsibilities slide first. It became easier and easier for her to neglect her routine chores at home, but she never became comfortable about the neglect. Instead her discomfort drove her deeper into her lethargy. She rarely slept more than five hours a night, and reached a state of mental numbness where she felt she could go on forever without sleeping or without getting any more tired or without any difference in the way she felt. It was as if she were always walking in three feet of water so that every motion was infinitely slowed but required extra exertion which completely exhausted her, while allowing her to accomplish little.

For the first thirty seconds or so each morning after she awoke she felt stable. Then like an avalanche descended on her, it hit her that she was the same old Helen, going to face the same old problems, with the same inadequacy with which she had faced them the day before and the day before that. Thus she had thirty seconds of peace each waking day. It wasn't enough.

Her children returned from camp but she was barely aware of it except it meant there was more required of her. It took her a week to do the laundry they brought back.

With a will of iron she used all her resources to keep up at the office. She drove the Lincoln to work each day, and this action neither diminished nor augmented her anxiety for she now knew that the "scares" were not connected with the car. It seemed a long, long time ago that she had purchased it.

During this three weeks she sought help in various forms. She telephoned her mother long distance, but was able to make only inconsequential small talk with her. She found out she could not ask her mother for help nor indeed imply that she needed it. It was no different when her father came on the line, and she concluded the long distance conversation by assuring them that her family were "all just fine" and she had "just wanted to say hello." Several close friends called her because they hadn't heard from her, but their interest and concern increased her jitters and she could hardly wait until she could hang up politely.

She took up practicing the piano, an activity she had given up when she quit college. She attempted to "play out" her emotions, much as she had done successfully during her youth. She felt better when she played, but her skills were rusty and she found herself frustrated at her poor technique.

She lost five pounds. Wishfully hoping this weight loss indicated an explainable disease or illness, she went to her family physician for a complete checkup. When he finished the tests he said, "Everything seems to be fine. I don't think your five-pound weight loss is very significant." In a more personal tone he added, "Helen, you do look terribly tired and strained. I don't find a thing in your tests to account for it. Is there anything that's troubling you that you'd like to talk about?"

Her first impulse was to unburden herself and cry on his shoulder, pouring out her misery and bafflement at what was happening to her. The words she uttered were, "Oh, heavens no, Dr. Gardner. Everything's just fine. It's just the end-of-summer drearies. Don't you think everyone in Phoenix feels this way the last few hot weeks of August?" She had managed to keep her voice light, her sole object being to get out of there. She fled to the car, barely making it before the shaking began again and the next "scare" enveloped her.

In a final attempt to cope with what she now continually thought of as her "madness," she went to the public library and checked her limit of four books: *The Psychology of Women* by Helen Deutch; *The Neurotic Personality of Our Time* by Karen Horney; and Sigmund Freud's *Interpretation of Dreams* and *Collected Papers*. She skipped the parts she didn't comprehend at all and devoured the portions she even vaguely understood as if the process of reading them would cure her. Every symptom she read about seemed to apply to her. She read them on her lunch hours and until nearly dawn each morning, going to the office a little more haggard each day.

She returned the books to the public library the following week and, being embarrassed to check out any more books on the same subject because she thought the librarian had looked at her strangely, the following Saturday she drove into nearby Scottsdale to their library, bringing home with her: *Language and Thought in Schizophrenia* by Kasanan; *Recognizing the Depressed Patient* by Ayd; *Textbook of Psychiatry* by Henderson and Gillespie; and *Depression* by Beck.

Continuing her do-it-yourself campaign against the "scares," she buried herself in these books. The result was that she became familiar with psychological and psychiatric terms and that she initially felt

relieved because she was at least doing something con-
structive, and finally that she progressively felt worse.
She did not realize until later than an intellectual
understanding of emotional problems was a far cry
from alleviating her own unstable thinking. The only
difference now was that she no longer thought of herself as having "my madness" or a "scare"; she was
intermittently according to her prevailing mood
"manic-depressive," "schizophrenic," "psychot-
ically-depressed," and on her very best days "mildly
neurotic."

Her energy was now spent almost exclusively in
attempting to appear normal to the world. In this effort she succeeded better than she realized.

A great deal of the time she felt as if she were
standing in knee-deep quicksand watching a thirty
foot wall of water rushing towards her. She combated
these sensations by telling herself: "That wall of water
won't hit for at least thirty minutes. I'll have time to
finish this report first." She operated on the principle
of "half an hour at a time." To all outward appear-
ances she carried on her duties much as she had before
and was continually astonished that the world in
general did not detect her true state of mind. To her
husband she seemed to be "more irritable than usual."
To her children, who were involved in their own
affairs and the excitement of returning to school, she
was "crabby and picky," but the same old Mom. To
her boss, Tom, she appeared "tired and strained and
not getting enough sleep." She continued to play the
piano, sometimes with tears streaming down her face,

trying to express her emotions and thereby rid herself of them, but she could not "play them away."

(It would be so much easier if I had an obvious—to the world—reason to look and feel as if I had been hit by a truck. Dark glasses hiding red-rimmed, swollen eyes and a dejected appearance are so much more excusable and understandable if one has been dealt a blow which all the world can understand—loss of a loved one, your house burned down, incurable disease. It is so difficult for me because I have no obvious reason for feeling this way and there is absolutely no one whom I can tell: "You see, I seem to have fallen into a trap. It is an invisible trap, so you cannot see how well I am caught in it. I have been in it for what seems forever—enough time that it has robbed me of any sense of well-being and of my faith in my own judgment and perspective." It would be very nice if I could go to Steve. One does not go to one's husband with such cheery bits of information, though, does one? There are some husbands one does not even go to for five dollars, let alone say, "Listen to the details of my madness.")

A month after the day Helen had bought her Lincoln—the day the first payment was due—she reviewed the past thirty days, as she drove home from the office. (A month! A whole month I have lived this way! Now I have twenty-nine payments left on this car. Will each of those months be like this past one? If they are, there is no way I can possibly live through it.)

As she had this last thought she noticed she was

almost in front of St. Thomas Catholic Church. On a
sudden impulse she swerved sharply into the church's
parking lot, causing the man in the car behind her to
use some extremely un-Christian language and an
elderly priest, who had the misfortune of being in her
path, to become surprisingly nimble. She managed a
sickly, apologetic smile at the priest, secretly admir-
ing his agility, but wondering if she had already
blown it with God, too.

Neither Helen nor any of her family were Catholics. She had no idea why St. Thomas Catholic Church
should unexpectedly seem to be a last refuge to her.
She did have that Protestant knowledge that Catholic churches were "always open," and remembered
she would need something to cover her head. Or had
that been changed? Better not take a chance. Casting
about wildly for something which would be suitable,
her eyes fell on the box of Kleenex on the dashboard.
Unhesitatingly she pulled one from the box and
pinned it to her head with two bobby pins. She took
no time to inspect the effect of her improvisation; her
salvation was too near at hand to concern herself. To
her relief the church was completely empty.

She entered on tiptoe. Her anxiety temporarily
left her in the confusion she felt about ritual and etiquette. She tried to remember what the Kennedys
had done when they entered the church for the President's funeral. Glancing about her quickly to be certain no one was lurking unseen in the shadows, she
hurried down the aisle.

She tried to pray, but she was distracted by the

elaborate altar and the statues, all of which seemed to be looking directly at her. She closed her eyes but could still see their faces with expressions somewhere between serene contempt and arrogant pity. She opened her eyes and watched the flickering shadows cast by candles lit near the altar. She had sought solace and found further terror. (What am I doing here? What a strange place for me to be. What did I think I would find here?) The statues, the fragrance of incense, the flickering candles, and the deadly quiet all blended into an urgent desire to flee. No longer attempting to be quiet, she ran down the aisle, her shoes clattering in the silence. She fled the church as if pursued, leaving one torn white Kleenex unnoticed behind her.

She walked directly past her car and crossed the street to a bar whose neon sign blinked "The Haven." She ordered a double scotch on the rocks and downed it wordlessly. Her last magical hope of conquering the "scares" was shattered.

Thus, one month and one day after her first anxiety attack she made an appointment with Dr. Odell.

Chapter 5

As Helen entered Dr. Odell's waiting room for the first time, her stride was brisk and confident, the utter reverse of her fearful and uncertain state of mind. Helen's tactics in handling any uneasiness about a new situation had always been to appear as if she were an old hand at this sort of thing. With a flourish of self-assurance she took a seat in the waiting room and opened a magazine. She mentally rehearsed her previously contrived story. In the event she should meet anyone she knew, she planned to say that she had come by this office to pick up some important legal papers for her boss.

She purposely left on her dark glasses, not so much because she actually believed they disguised her from recognition but because they offered her a sense of protection. Protection from what, she wasn't sure. It was very nearly an adult form of the childhood game of clapping both hands over the eyes, proclaiming, "I can see you but you can't see me." Her dark glasses had seen heavy duty in the last few weeks.

(I'm sweating like a damned plow horse. I wish I could go home and shower and start all over. Damn it! Of all times I wanted to appear calm, cool, and collected and try to present a semblance of self-containment, and I'm going to have to meet this doctor when I'm looking wilted and sticky and clammy. I wish the hell I hadn't come. How will I ever explain to him what's wrong with me? I won't be able to find words, and even if I do, will it make sense to him? I wonder what he is like. He had a nice voice. Probably just his telephone voice he uses to lure lost souls into his lair. No, that isn't fair. He sounded more like a gentle, kindly, soft-spoken older man —maybe even a white-haired grandfather? Except that maybe he can read my mind. I must remember to think clean thoughts for the next hour. If I don't think about sex or bring up the subject, maybe he won't either. That's supposed to be their prime interest. I must begin to sort out what I will tell him and what I won't. Where the hell is he anyway? He's already two minutes late. All the books said they were so prompt.)

When Dr. Odell walked into the waiting room to greet his new patient, he was pleasantly surprised to see an attractive, well-put-together brunette neatly groomed, wearing a bright-colored summer dress. He breathed a small sigh of relief, happily contrasting this woman with the image he had conjured up from their phone conversation. From her tearful, desperate tone of voice during her phone call to make the appointment, he had expected to encounter an older, slumped, matronly woman wearing ill-fitting dark clothes and having a lined, woebegone face. Attractive women were more fun, and depressed patients often presented immediate life or death decisions and strained his schedule to work in extra hours. As he approached her, he was a bit startled to see that this feminine woman appeared to be engrossed in a copy of *Mechanix Illustrated*.

"I'm Dr. Odell," he said. "Are you Mrs. James?"

"Yes. Yes, I am, Doctor." (He isn't what I expected. White-haired grandfather indeed! Why, he can't be much older than I am.)

"I'm sorry to be a little late. I usually run on time. Come on in," he said, pointing the way into his office.

Helen laid down her unread magazine and led the way into the doctor's office, getting inside the door before she realized she had left her purse in the waiting room. Flustered, she hurried back to receive it, apologizing, and feeling her sense of dignity dented. (I am behaving like a school girl. Leaving my purse and rushing around like a silly teen-ager.)

Dr. Odell appeared not to notice the flurry of activity in Helen's forgetting and then retrieving her purse. But he did mentally reasses her, thinking to himself that her initial appearance of calmness might be deceiving. He smiled encouragingly at her as she walked past him into the office and seated herself in the chair he indicated. He sat down at his desk chair and took up pad and pencil. He did this slowly, as he sensed Helen needed a moment or two to organize herself.

"I'd better write down a few things about you here, or we might not get to it," Dr. Odell said. He had found through experience that getting to the vital statistics on a new patient at the beginning of the first hour helped to give the patient a little breathing space and himself a beginning idea of the patient's life situation. It seemed in his experience that the familiar act of simply giving one's name, address, age, and family members helped break the ice between himself and his patient, and also gave him an idea of the type of person with whom he was working.

He remembered one occasion earily in his practice when an anxious, hysterical, and verbal young woman had burst into his office for her first appointment, blurting out her emotional difficulties almost before she was seated. It took him half the session to learn that she was a nun. That information *did* make a difference.

"All right, Doctor. What do you want to know?" (I know what he wants to know. Name and address so he will know where to send the bill! Or else he wants to get my name down because I'm such a nonentity he's sure he'll forget me the moment I get out the door. Oh, God, how did I ever get into this mess anyway. Nothing about this place suggests even a remote glimmer of hope in discovering what's causing my "scares.")

"Let's start with your name and address."

"Helen James; 3020 Saddleback Lane." (I feel like a captive. Name, rank, and serial number. Isn't that all a prisoner has to give?)

"Is that Phoenix or Scottsdale?"

"Phoenix. Just barely. Zip Code 85018."

"What is your husband's first name?"

"Steven. Steven F. James," she answered. (I feel as if I'm applying either for a job or a bank loan.)

"How long have you been married?"

"Fifteen years." (Here it comes. How is my sex life? Do I have orgasms? Do I like sex? I know what all the next questions are going to be.)

"Have either of you been married before?"

"No, neither of us." (My crystal ball is malfunctioning today. He is going to be circuitous. I know my lines with Steven, but this is a new play.)

"Do you have children?"

"Yes, two." (And how did I get them? Through sex. Now he's going to start.)

"Boys or girls?"

"One of each. My daughter, Valerie, is thirteen, and my son, Andrew—Andy—will be eleven in a couple of months. They're really great kids."

Dr. Odell observed a note of enthusiasm. Helen had volunteered her first bit of information in discussing her children, for the first time expressing a real feeling rather than a bare fact. He began to eliminate the idea of a mother-child problem.

"Are they doing all right in school?" he asked, partly to verify his impression that her children were not her problem and partly to allow her to expand on what was apparently a safe topic for her.

"Beautifully. Both of them. They make good grades—mostly A's and B's—and they like school. I guess that probably helps, doesn't it?" She smiled. She was happy to report about her children, for in motherhood she did not feel like a failure. It was far easier to discuss her achievements than her problems.

(I'd like to tell him that my problem child is the third one—my thirty-six-year-old husband who is parading in disguise as a man.)

"I agree. It helps to like what you are doing. Do they like the other kids, too?"

"They drag other kids home in gangs. I assume they like them. Andy gets into a fight with the boy down the street a couple of times a year, but they always settle their differences and become friends again." (Maybe I should tell him that my husband and I fight regularly about every two weeks and we are never friends in between. Doesn't he want to know about me? Is he a child psychologist? I feel as if I'm having a conference with one of the kids' teachers.)

"Is it easier for you to fight with them or love them?"

"Oh, far easier to love them. Sometimes when they misbehave—which they do, I admit—it is very difficult for me to punish them. I do it because I know it is necessary, but it is always with the idea of getting the punishment over so we can be friends again. I guess that term, 'friends,' really applies to how I feel about them. I enjoy their company and I just feel better when they are both at home. They are both quite affectionate. My son is getting to the age where I get a hug only on occasions when nobody else is within sight. I suppose he sees it quite unmanly to be

caught with an arm around Mom. Valerie is not quite
so demonstrative as Andy. Seldom does she hug me or
Steve, but she does things like hide little poems she
has written so I will find them when I brush my teeth,
or sometimes she will surprise us on Sunday morning
by fixing breakfast and having it all on the table before
she wakes us up. Since Steve and I sleep like rocks on
the weekend, this isn't difficult," she added with a
smile.

Dr. Odell's smile was amused and understanding. "Your kids sound fine," he said. "How is your
health? Do you have any health problems?"

"No." (Certainly not, Doctor, unless of course
you would consider headaches, insomnia, dizziness,
frigidity, lack of appetite, intermittent blurring
vision, and various applicable psychological symptoms in those damned books to be health problems.)

Dr. Odell thought to himself that her response
was the shortest and fastest health summary he had
ever heard. A simple and succinct "no." Maybe it was
not so simple. He did not, however, confront her with
the brevity of her answer.

"Nothing like headaches, stomach aches, digestive trouble?"

"An occasional headache maybe," she said. (But
no more than any other mental patient.)

He inquired into the frequency, length, duration,
and type of headaches and got a minimum of information. He began to wonder why she seemed so sensitive
and withholding about health. He decided to avoid
probing further and to move on to another topic. Per-

haps he could get a medical report from her family physician.

"Incidentally, who is your family physician?"

"Well, he—why do you want to know?" she asked warily. (The medical fraternity—I suppose he wants to get together with Dr. Gardner so they can discuss my symptoms and maybe my sex life. Pretty soon the whole medical society will know I'm crazy. I'd as soon keep the fact of my failings from Dr. Gardner.)

"I was thinking about saving time and effort in getting your medical history," he answered, trying to allay her obvious suspicions. "But if you have some reservations, we'll let it go for now. I won't contact anyone without your permission."

"I'm sorry to be so cautious. One of my problems these days seems to be not wanting to confide anything to anybody."

"I don't really expect instant trust," he said. "In fact I might be a little suspicious myself if it ever happened," he added, smiling. "But if it helps, I want to assure you that whatever you tell me is strictly confidential and will never go beyond this room."

Helen crossed and uncrossed her legs and lit her third cigarette. Paradoxically these gestures did not denote an increase in her anxiety but a slight lessening, for up to this point she had been rigid and unmoving in her chair. She had not removed her dark glasses.

Dr. Odell noticed that she had relaxed a barely perceptible amount. He deliberately allowed a short pause with the hope she might volunteer her problem. If this highly anxious woman could begin to direct the hour more herself, she would feel in better control and less threatened. She did not fulfill his hope but continued to behave like a witness being cross-examined.

"Are you a housewife or do you have a job?" he asked.

"I'm a legal secretary," she said, almost as if she were ashamed of it. (Of course I never intended to be a legal secretary. Or a housewife! But I seem to be both. I intended to be the greatest living concert pianist the world has ever known. I had such unattainable aims. I feel silly admitting them to myself anymore.)

"Full time?"

"Yes, five days a week. I've been at my present job four years."

"Do you like your job?"

She hesitated only a moment. "Yes, I suppose I do. I have a really great boss. He hired me with absolutely no experience in legal work, and with his help I've become a pretty acceptable secretary." (Why did I say that? He didn't accuse me of being a lousy secretary. A lousy wife, maybe. A lousy lay lately. But a damned good secretary and typist. And why not? Hands that spent five hours a day practicing Bach all those years ought to be able to handle a simple typewriter.)

Dr. Odell was curious about her apologetic tone of voice in describing her work, as if she were confessing to being a scrub woman. It was always a temptation for him to pry further when a patient's tone of voice and facial expression did not fit his spoken words. In this instance, her apologetic tone of voice and self-disparaging expression were in contrast with her response that she liked her job and had a great boss. He did not press further, however, because he did not want to frighten her away by forcing her to look at her hidden feelings before she trusted him.

"Were you trained for any other job?" he asked her, attempting to get the information he wanted but still trying to stay on safe ground.

"No, not for a job actually." She smiled. "You will laugh at this. I never studied typing in school. I went to college and majored in music and had grandiose plans to be a concert pianist. Even my shorthand is fake—it's just an abbreviated form of longhand that only I can read." (See there, Doctor. I can even laugh at myself. I can't be all bad.)

"I never laugh at high aspirations," he said. "I am pleased that you told me about your music. And maybe you could call yourself inventive rather than a faker."

"I'll admit I like your word better than I do mine," Helen answered. (He's really rather nice. Maybe he won't be as difficult to talk to as I thought.)

"Have you kept up with the piano at all?"

"Oh, no, not for years," she said. "At least not until recently. The last few weeks I've played more than I have in ten years—so much that my husband is complaining."

"What does he complain about?"

"My timing. By the time I do the dishes and get the kids to bed, it's late, and that's the only time I have to practice. He says I keep him awake," she lied. (What he really says is that I stay up playing the piano to avoid going to bed with him. And what he really says is true.)

Dr. Odell thought privately that Helen obviously was avoiding sex by choosing late hours to practice.

"Does your husband complain about other things?" he asked. "Does he have something to do with why you came to see me today?" By asking the two separate questions, he tried to ease her into discussing her real reason for coming in. If she were ready she could answer his second query. If not, she could respond only to the question about her husband's complaints.

"I honestly don't know if he has anything to do with it or not," Helen answered. "We don't have the best marriage in the world, but nothing has changed to make me feel as bad as I have the last few weeks."

"How have you been feeling lately?"

"I don't know how to describe it," she answered, and her voice quaked. Tears began to run down her cheeks and from beneath the dark glasses. (Damn it! I'm going to sit here and bawl. I don't even have any Kleenex. I should have known I'd lose control in here and stuffed my purse with them.)

Dr. Odell silently handed her a Kleenex.

"Thank you," she said, thinking how difficult it was to wipe her eyes with dark glasses on. "I'm sorry to sniffle around like this. I'm not usually such a baby. I just don't understand what's been happening to me." (What a disgusting mess I am. I wish I were anyplace else in the world right now. I wonder if he thinks I really am crazy. I wonder if I am crazy myself.)

"Don't fight the tears in here," he said. Actually he was heartened by her weeping. This was not because he liked to see her suffer, but because it is usually a healthy, human sign of feeling. He worried more about the cold, unresponsive patients who could not cry. "This is a special place where crying is encouraged. It's really hard to fight tears and to think at the same time," he said.

"It's so difficult to have someone seeing me being so weak. It makes me feel ridiculous and that makes me angry." She blew her nose and wiped her eyes again.

"Well, I don't think crying is weak or ridiculous."

"That's because you're not crying," she said. (Oh, I'll just bet you don't think it's weak. I have never felt so defenseless. Or weak. Or vulnerable.)

"I, too, was raised to believe that it was weak to cry. But I have changed my mind. I have cried, and I've felt better afterwards."

Helen looked at him to see if he really meant it or was saying this to make her feel better. (He looks so sincere. I've never heard a man admit that he cried before. I can't imagine Steve crying. Or admitting to it if he did. I suppose that just makes Dr. Odell a weaker man than Steve. Only it doesn't seem that way to me. Dr. Odell doesn't look weak at all. Oh, how I wish I could tell him about all these feelings that have been slowly killing me. I'm just afraid to start because I'm so upset I don't know what will come out if I let myself begin.)

"It sounds as if you are recommending an old-fashioned 'good cry.' I have never understood that phrase. I guess it is because I have only 'bad cries.' I never remember in my life feeling better after crying. It usually takes me a couple of days to claw my way back out of the quagmire when I really let go." Tears still streamed out from under the dark glasses.

"I guess you're right. People really do cry for different reasons and with different results. Maybe we can make these tears turn out differently."

"I don't really understand what you mean, but your saying it makes me feel better." (Thank God he didn't sympathize with me or tell me I had every right to cry when I feel so bad. I think the least bit of sympathy at this point would put me into such a well of self-pity I would never get out. But neither did he tell me to dry my eyes and be a big girl. Somehow I expected either sympathy or condemnation for my tears. I wonder if *he* knew what he meant.)

"Was that a main reason you came to see me because you have been crying a lot lately?" He doubted that this was actually the reason but it was a way to introduce the all-important question: Why had she come? The timing of his question was dictated both by professional skill and considerable personal curiosity.

"No, although it certainly is true I have cried a

lot. I guess the main reason is I don't know why I am crying. That's not the worst. What is really the worst is that I think I am losing my mind." (Oh, where are the words to describe to him what happened that day in the office when I had my first "scare." Please, please let me communicate.)

"I'm having trouble trying to describe—'attacks' is the only word I can think of. I have thought of them myself as 'scares.' Because I actually felt afraid. But it didn't make any sense to me because I didn't know what I was afraid of. I don't know why I am using the past tense here. I still feel afraid and I still don't know the source of the fear. I couldn't feel more frightened if I were pursued by evil, hairy monsters. Since this obviously isn't the case—I haven't seen a hairy monster in at least a week," she threw in, trying to minimize the enormity of her confession by making light of it, "the only explanation I can think of is that my mind is playing tricks on me. That's the most tolerable way I can think of to say I'm going crazy. I feel so alone inside my head. No one I know has ever described feeling anything like this." She paused to gauge his reaction.

"Now, you say the worst part is having some kind of attacks—like fear—and the feeling that you are going to lose your mind?" he asked, rephrasing Helen's own words. "Already just from being around you and having seen a lot of genuinely crazy people, I strongly suspect that you are not crazy and are not likely to become crazy." He was aware that Helen's anxiety was probably at the root of her suspicion of

being crazy, and he hastened to assure her as un-
qualifiedly as he could that this was not the case.

"It is the fearful feelings that make you feel as if
you are crazy?" he asked.

"Yes, that's exactly it. Most of the time, even
when I feel low and depressed, I still feel quite sane,"
she answered. "But when I have one of these 'scares'
—that's still the word that seems to fit them best—it
is as if my thinking becomes irrational. My thoughts
chase one another around in circles, gaining speed all
the time, but they seem to lack any sort of continuity
or sense. Would you like me to tell you about the first
time it happened?"

"Please do," he nodded. "When was it?"

"I don't think I could describe this to you had
you not just assured me you don't think I'm crazy,"
Helen said. "Those were comforting words. It was
about a month ago. One month and three days actually, so you see I can pinpoint the time exactly. I don't
think I ever will forget the first time I had one of my
attacks. Shall I start at the beginning of the attack, or
shall I start with what happened before what I think
brought it on?"

"Start with what happened before," he said. He
had learned that telling a patient to start anywhere he
wished or to do with the hour as he pleased, which
seemed like invitations to freedom, often served to
remind the patient that he was a patient and forced
him to make a choice when he was already having
enough trouble with choices.

"It happened on a Wednesday the first time," she

began, and she related the fight with Steve on the Tuesday night before. She described the argument about the airplane and Steve's stomping out of the house, leaving her a "forlorn winner," as she put it. She told him about how her car had failed to start the next morning and the thoughts she had had about her marriage and her car disintegrating simultaneously.

"I felt that I had to do something—anything— even if it was the wrong thing," she continued, that might make me feel better. I really date the beginning of my 'scares' with that morning my car wouldn't start. I couldn't concentrate after I got to the office, and all I could think of was that Steve wanted to take all our money and buy a plane and let me continue driving that beat-up old rattletrap forever. Now that I'm telling you about it, it just doesn't make sense to me that such a simple thing could cause such a turbulence in my head." (I'm not saying it right. Damn it, he probably doesn't understand my feelings about it any more than Steve did. I saw him look at the clock. He's bored to death and wants nothing more than for this hour to end.)

"It's pretty important to believe your feelings," Dr. Odell said. "What may sound like a 'simple thing' can lead to very painful and complicated feelings. Rarely is it truly a simple thing that causes anxiety attacks, and from your description I would say that's what you have been having. Try to tell me more specifically how you actually feel during one of your 'scares.' "

"I really don't even like to think about them

when I'm not having one. I am thankful for the mere fact it's gone for the present. Is that what you really think they are? Anxiety attacks?" (What did those damned books say about anxiety? Being afraid and not knowing the source of the fear. That's what I've got, all right.)

"I *think* they are, but I'd like to hear a little more description about what happens to you when you have one." He decided she could tolerate a little more firmness now, and he would not let her get by with evading his direct question of favor of definitions.

"It is like a sudden and unpredictable sense of foreboding. I'm getting the feeling now. I hope you're not bringing one of them on. Although maybe it wouldn't be such a bad idea. Perhaps I could describe one of the attacks better if I were in the middle of one. God forbid."

"You don't need to go that far," he said, smiling. "Go on."

"Well, there is this sense of dread, as I say. But no matter how bad the feeling of dread and foreboding is, I feel that it is only a taste of what is to come, that I haven't gone through the worst of it yet. There is no indication of its going away so that I can tell myself to be patient and outwait it. Suddenly I will break out in a sweat and my heart beats faster, as if my entire body is preparing for a desperate chase. I feel that my mind is sending signals to my body to get ready to run and at the same time conveying the message that it will never be able to run fast enough. My entire be-ing behaves as though I were confronted face to face with a grizzly bear, adrenalin gushing and my whole system sort of speeded up. I'm sure I wouldn't respond much differently if there were a real danger confronting me. It is far more frightening to me because there is nothing real to threaten me," she said, the words rushing out.

"Come on now, Dr. Odell, you have to admit that that sounds pretty, well, if not crazy, overdramatic and ridiculous." (Now I've done it. I've given him enough documentation to put me away forever. I've told him too much.) She was glad she had never removed her dark glasses because now she actively studied Dr. Odell, watching his face closely for any indication that he had changed his mind about classifying her as noncrazy.

"It certainly doesn't sound ridiculous, and I know that you are often in great pain. You may be overly dramatic in other circumstances, but when you describe intense anxiety, it is vivid and to the point. It's pretty easy for you to feel that you're exaggerating, because you don't even want to believe it yourself."

"I suppose." (Now he is pacifying me. I'll bet he'd say the same thing even if he did think I was crazy. I've given him too much ammunition. I should have bitten off my tongue before I blurted out all my symptoms. Now that I've told him, they all sound like a great bundle of nonsense anyway. Maybe everyone has such crazy feelings from time to time, and the only difference with me is that I couldn't keep my mouth shut about them.)

"You sound a bit dubious," Dr. Odell said. Her tone of voice had changed abruptly and her face had become impassive. She had subtly moved back further in her chair and resumed her initial businesslike manner. There were no tears now.

"You seem to have turned off," he said when she made no response.

"I'm not sure what you mean. I have answered every question you have asked me to the best of my ability." She lit another cigarette and behaved as if she were nearing the end of a dull PTA meeting.

Dr. Odell knew now that she had emotionally withdrawn and that she felt very defensive and threatened. He felt mildly frustrated that he could not deal with these feelings directly, but knew that for the time being the barrier between them had been secured. He saw this happen every day to a small or to a great extent when a patient had felt he had said too much and regretted it immediately. It was sometimes exasperating to him that therapy had to be so slow and tedious. However, it took time to assure a patient that he wasn't going to be rejected because of this inner feeling. It was always the doctor's temptation to move in too quickly, emotionally. He almost gave up the effort to restore the closer communication of a few moments ago, but doggedly made one more try, knowing that some people found it easier to talk of feelings felt in the past rather than feelings felt in the present.

"Tell me this; do you remember having any feelings like these 'scares' before you met your husband?"

"No, definitely not," was Helen's immediate, too-quick response. (Why should that question make me feel trapped? Of course, I've never had these feelings before. Wouldn't anyone remember if he thought he was losing his mind? Except that somehow it touches a nerve. There was that summer between high school and college. No, that couldn't have anything to do with my problems now. I suppose that he is now going to delve into my childhood, which seems absurd in light of the fact that my troubles started one month ago. Oh, God. I just want out of this place.)

Dr. Odell was beginning to feel irritated with Helen. He wanted to shake her and say: You can do better than this. What happened to you back there? What went on inside your head that turned you from a worried but warm human into an impersonal, denying stranger?

"We have about ten minutes left," Dr. Odell said, glancing at his office clock. "Let me get a little more of your background. Do you have any brothers or sisters?"

"One brother. Three years younger than I."

Repeated questions as to the details of the relationship between Helen and her brother yielded practically nothing. The same was true of queries concerning her parents ("Living and well"), her religion ("Weak Protestant"), and her childhood ("uneventfully pleasant").

As Dr. Odell announced the end of the session, he picked up his appointment book. "Shall we make another appointment?" he asked.

"I don't exactly know my schedule right now. May I check my calendar at the office and call you?" (Wild horses wouldn't drag me back in here. I wouldn't commit myself to another session like today under threats of torture. At least I have it from the horse's mouth that I'm not crazy. And that's all I wanted to know.)

"You did say over the phone that your fee is thirty dollars an hour, didn't you?" she asked.

"That's right."

"Will you bill me?"

Dr. Odell was convinced she had decided not to come back again and felt helpless to do anything about it.

"That's my usual procedure," he said, rising from his chair and leading Helen toward the door. "Call as soon as you can," he added. "I hope this first hour hasn't jangled your nerves too much."

"Oh, no," she said, almost gaily, with freedom in sight as he opened the door. "Actually, I feel much better. Good-by."

Dr. Odell nodded his head and waved, but he did not say good-by. As she walked out of his waiting room, he wondered idly what color her eyes were. She had never removed the dark glasses. Maybe she never would and he would never know.

Thus Dr. Odell was surprised, almost amazed in fact when Helen called him the next day requesting another appointment. He agreed to see her the same time the following week. Ever the optimist, and remembering her reticence and defensiveness of the day before, he closed their phone conversation by saying, "Please write me a little more detailed history about your early life. I'd be interested in anything you can remember, even if it seems trivial to you. Specifically about your immediate family, your brother and your parents. Some people do think and remember better when they are by themselves, and sometimes it is easier to organize your thoughts when you are writing rather than talking."

"Will it save me money, too?" she asked, the warm, good-natured tone back in her voice. "Because I have figured out that it costs me sixty cents a minute to talk to you. I'd feel as if every word I write is money in the bank," she laughed.

"It's the one sure way to be a paid author," he said in the same vein. He felt good when he hung up.

She's pretty brave on the telephone, he thought. I doubt if she will write so bravely.

He was glad she was coming back.

Chapter 6

Three days later Dr. Odell received a legal-sized envelope bearing Helen's return address in the corner. He was totally unprepared for the sheer volume of material which it contained. In his short break between patients he glanced curiously at the first page, but the pressure of his schedule forced him to put it aside until later. He came back early from lunch to read Helen's history. It actually looked like a manuscript, in that it was neatly typed and double spaced on heavy bond paper. He began to read, hoping that it would be interesting even though it appeared gruesomely long.

Dear Doctor Odell:

As to your request for a family history, I approach the project with feelings somewhere between those negative ones I had when assigned a similar task in the eighth grade and flattery that anyone would be interested in my "autobiography." Thus part of me rebels at disclosing any more than necessary for a "passing grade" and part of me wishes to embellish and exaggerate my good deeds and attributes and delete any negative qualities which might detract from this recorded history. Perhaps I will hit a happy medium.

I am not exactly sure what information you want to know about me, but I assume it is more than what you could glean from the Vital Statistics Bureau. I shall write down facts and memories as they occur to me, and you may feel free to collate them in your own mind as you read.

Steve is at a dinner meeting this evening, and the children are both in bed. They spent the evening with friends so I got out of cooking dinner and feasted on a peanut butter sandwich and a glass of milk. This for some reason reminded me of my junior year of high school when my mother had major surgery and entrusted the care of my father and brother to me. As I recall, my brother took some of his ill-gotten funds (most of which was probably interest I had paid him on loans, for he always had money and I never did) and simply ate at hamburger joints. This left me with Daddy. (Note, Doctor: she still calls her father "Daddy.")

If this wasn't a case of the blind leading the blind, I never saw one. My poor father is absolutely dependent upon my mother when it has anything to do with the kitchen, and he would literally starve if left to his own devices. I tempted him with such delicacies as—again—peanut butter sandwiches, cans of cold pork and beans, lumpy potato soup (canned), hard fried eggs with the yolks broken, and several un-

*recognizable, burnt items. He never once complained,
and while he certainly didn't comment on the superb
quality of the cuisine, he nevertheless seemed to recognize that I was trying—which I really was. My father
would nearly die of starvation before he would eat
out—he hates restaurants—but I believe this is one
time he strongly considered the idea. The rather
pained expression left his eyes when my mother returned home and took over in the kitchen again.*

   *But the whole point of this is that I really didn't
feel as inept during that situation as I still do to this
day when I work in the kitchen with my mother. We
just don't do things in the same way. (We certainly
didn't learn in the same place. She learned from her
mother. I learned by myself, for my mother was certain that my delicate hands were destined for far
greater glories than those of the kitchen, and whenever I would ask her, "How did you bake that pie?"
or "What do you put in white sauce?" she responded
by telling me to "Run along and practice the piano
now, and I'll just finish up here in the kitchen.")
Last December my parents came to visit me, and
while they were here I nearly cut off a finger, managed
to burn my hand while taking a roast out of the oven,
broke several dishes, and probably would have
severed a limb had they stayed for the winter.*

   *Last Thanksgiving Day I had fourteen people for
dinner, and I didn't have the least bit of trouble. I did
have a few moments of panic while preparing the meal
and wondered what had possessed me to invite them
all, but it turned out quite well, and with much less*

confusion than is usually present in my mother's holiday kitchen.

When I am working in the kitchen with my mother during her visits to see us, she continually tells me how well I am doing and "Isn't that a pretty salad mold," when it is all sloping to one side like a sinking ship, or "Here, let me do that for you. You have worked all day." I have the feeling she wonders how Valerie and Andy got so healthy and never have colds and don't have a cavity in their heads, since I, their poor inadequate mother, obviously cannot bake a potato.

The end result is that I simply leave the kitchen for the duration of my parents' stay and let mother fuss over all of us while I drink beer with my father— lead him astray, I am sure is my mother's opinion. And Daddy then winks at me as if to say, "You know your mother is never happy unless she is fussing over all of us, and you are wise to let her have the kitchen to herself." My kitchen. Then, after they leave and go back to Denver, I take a Saturday and put all the dishes and pots and pans back where they belong and broil everything for a month, since my mother never broils anything "because it makes such a mess." And that is the Betty Crocker section of my family history.

Dr. Odell paused in his reading. For a moment he felt appreciative of Helen's sense of humor and humanness. At a more evaluative level he noted the masochism in her humor, her tendency to intellectualize, her probable minimizing of problems, and the wealth of unconsciously significant Oedipal material.

He felt a twinge of dislike for Helen's mother whose seemingly generous behavior served as a rationalization for her covert, hostile possessiveness of the woman's role in the family.

He continued to read.

As you requested, I have been trying to think about my relationship with my brother, Craig. I can't seem to remember much about him. Isn't that strange? When we were home, we just pretty much went our separate ways as soon as we were old enough to do so, although I remember we argued a great deal when we were small. In retrospect, I don't suppose we fought any more than most kids. I do recall defending him when he was very little and someone picked on him or teased him, but then I probably turned around and picked on or teased him myself. My mother and father used to say that we scrapped—"like all kids" —but tended to stick together against outsiders.

Craig was always a "loner." He liked to "fix" things and was forever tearing apart cars or clocks or lawn mowers and then putting them back together. He is married now, is practical and lives within his means, is well liked, doesn't drink, smoke, or beat his wife, but isn't in the least a stuffed shirt.

He was in the Navy for four years before he was married and was stationed for two of them in Japan, and during that time we exchanged Christmas cards. I did not particularly miss him or worry about him, and I am sure the feeling was mutual. I got all the news about him from Mother's letters, in which she alternately worried about his being led astray by "some of those naughty soldiers," about his being washed out to sea by a typhoon, or being attacked and shot by "one of those unpredictable Orientals." There was no war on at the time, and I doubt if my mother would have survivied if there had been.

When Craig was discharged (very honorably, of course), Mother worried about the plane crashing in the ocean on its return. After he was released from the service, he obligingly moved to and settled in Denver, where he will undoubtedly stay the rest of his life dutifully eating Sunday dinner at Mother's table and making her proud forevermore, unlike her roving daughter.

I do recall vividly the many times my mother verbally and in her actions stressed the importance of "treating her children exactly alike." I am sure this was because of her own childhood and her mother's repeated declarations about the worthlessness of girls and the many merits of boys. My mother never gave either Craig or me anything when the other did not receive a gift too. This included birthdays. I got a present on his birthday, and he on mine. We were told many times how precious we both were and how we were both loved equally, etc., etc., etc. "The lady doth protest too much." My mother now does this with my own children. Andy gets a gift on Valerie's birthday and vice versa. I do not particularly approve of this.

Dr. Odell again turned away from the manuscript and thought over what he had read. He felt a pang of sympathy for Helen who surely was greatly confused by her mother's reactive denying behavior. It was quite obvious to him that Helen saw her brother as the successful rival for their mother's love and that she had never been convinced by her mother's repeated proclamations that they were "loved equally." He made a mental note to explore her awareness of hostility toward her brother in the future. Certainly Helen's mother practically made a career out of hiding, denying, and repressing hostility toward her family.

When I was a little girl, I was with my father as constantly as he would permit. I used to pester him unmercifully while he worked on the car in the garage, which was his favorite pastime. When he finally had had enough and wanted to get rid of me, he would blow the horn. This startled me, and I am sure that I pretended to be much more afraid than I was, and I would run to the house and stay for an hour or so. It was a little game we played. I must have been about three years old at the time, because it was before my brother was born.

If there was one person I would rather be with than my father it was my Grandpa Langley—my father's father. My grandparents lived just down the street from us. I was their only grandchild, and they just spoiled me rotten. I ran away from home to their house regularly. My grandfather was the only person in the world who would let me drink coffee and who treated me at the age of four as if I were completely grown up and could understand just about anything. He was a politician and was County Assessor for years and years. On election day he would take me with him to the polls so I could "vote." Apparently the restrictions were much looser in those days, because he would let me have a real ballot and I would mark it all up with childish scribbles and "vote for Grandpa." I can still remember his slapping his knee and saying I was "the youngest voter in all the County and the smartest, too!"

He was a handsome old gentleman—had thick white curly hair and was a rather dynamic person. He alternately shouted and roared, and laughed and slapped his knee, and I thought he must look just like God. He used to rock me and sing to me and I can remember he sang "Old Dan Tucker." His full name was Lawrence D. Langley, but no one ever knew what the "D" really stood for because he had told them for years it stood for "Democrat." The only thing he hated worse than Republicans were Catholics. He had a framed picture of F.D.R. in his living room, and I really loved to hear him snort and carry on about the unspeakable vices and practices of the Republicans and the Papists. He would turn over in his grave if he knew I am now a Republican.

My grandfather died when I was eleven years old. It was the first time I ever saw my father cry. The second time was when his mother died.

Dr. Odell felt refreshed by Helen's colorful description of her grandfather's personality and character and was relieved that someone had unequivocally and directly loved her even though he may have indulged her. He mentally began to give Grandfather a great deal of credit, thinking to himself how the genuine and unaffected love of one adult in a child's life can sometimes be the saving factor. Although Helen's father seemed to have loved her and given her attention, it was not enough to make up for her mother's subtle rejection so she turned to her grandparents.

My Grandma Langley was also one of my favorites. She was Grandpa's third wife, his first two having died—probably from a combination of having so many babies and his shouting. My father had many half brothers and half sisters whom I don't know. My father was Grandma's only child and thus Craig and I were her only real grandchildren.

My Grandma Langley probably never tipped the scales at 100 pounds in her entire life. She rather completely ignored Grandpa's roars or said, "Oh, pshaw, Lawrence," when he really got on a tear—particularly around election time. She was a completely good person. She was so teeny-tiny and very neat and quiet, but rather spunky, too. She and my dad always greeted each other by shaking their fist at one another. She died of cancer of the digestive system when I was thirteen. She lived with us during this time, and it horrified me to watch this. She never complained, and up until the last day she lived, she and Daddy shook their fists at one another, both pretending that nothing was wrong.

She weighed sixty-eight pounds when she died. I can remember thinking she would never bake me any more sugar cookies. I refused to go to the funeral.

*She always told me I could have her wedding ring
and it was given to me the night she died. I cried myself to sleep and slept with it clutched in my hand. I
still have the ring, and it means a great deal to me.*

*I tell you all this about my grandparents because
during my very young years I spent much time with
them, as they took care of me while my mother
worked. When I was about seven I had scarlet fever
and was quarantined at my grandparents' house. I
was delighted that I had to stay there until I was well.*

*One more thing I remember about my grand-
mother. Before she died, she was bedfast for nearly a
year, and my mother cared for her. I could not have
any friends over to visit me during this period. I can
remember complaining about this and feeling rather
angry about it. After she died, I remember feeling
very guilty about having complained.*

This portion of Helen's letter caused Dr. Odell
to stop and reflect on his memories of his own grandparents. His own grandfather had been a fiery Irishman who had sat at the kitchen table and eaten his
dessert before the start of the meal. Dr. Odell had
been a small boy at the time, and had considered his
grandfather's behavior extremely brave, in that he
risked his grandmother's wrath. His grandfather had
often emphasized his point of view by banging on the
kitchen table with his fist and shouting. "Hell's afire,"
causing dishes to rattle and fly. He thought that perhaps his grandfather and Helen's might have been
either the best of friends or the worst of enemies. He
read on.

Thus, it seems that I always have been closer to my father's side of the family. My mother's brothers were all farmers and cowboys and did not see anything worthwhile in anyone who could not milk a cow or run a herd. They always seemed quite foreign to me. My mother had one sister—I should say has, for she is still living, if you can call it that. She has been in the State Hospital for as long as I can remember. I vaguely remember her and she always frightened me.

Occasionally the family would go to the hospital and bring her home for weekend visits when I was very small. She was quite delusional. She spoke of the "red angels" and the "black angels" and all the spirits who talked to her and all the dead people she knew. It still makes my hair stand on end as I remember how I felt about this as a child. My mother tried to explain it to me, but only succeeded in planting such a fear of insanity in my mind that I grew panic stricken at the thought of driving by that hospital or having my aunt come to visit. I do not think my mother should have allowed her to talk to me when I was so small.

Sometimes I think perhaps that is what I fear so greatly when I have an anxiety attack—"that I will completely lose my senses." I think probably that aunt frightened me more when I was little than anything I can remember. I have seen her once or twice since I've been grown, and she really is quite pathetic and not in the least frightening—until I remember how I felt about her as a child.

It seems to me that I was taken to the State Hos-

pital a couple of times with my parents when they went to visit her, and I felt a very real terror of that place. This is something that I have never told anyone before. I thought that must be the worst thing in the world that could happen to anyone, and the pieces of conversation I heard about this aunt confirmed my belief. I do recall asking many questions about how she "got that way," but I was always hushed. It makes me anxious just to remember those fears—which I don't believe I have ever shaken. I never spoke to anyone about them, but I can remember sitting numb with terror as she told me about her "spirits." I was about five years old.

Dr. Odell began to pull together some of the facts in Helen's letter with her behavior during their session. From these early experiences with her psychotic aunt, it was certainly understandable that she should have an excess of fear even though she fit the general category of a modern, well-educated, sophisticated person. He noted her admission that she had never spoken to anyone about her childhood fears of insanity. She apparently had not been encouraged as a child to be open about her feelings, rather she had been admonished and "hushed" when unacceptable topics were mentioned.

I was an awful show-off as a child. The Christmas night when I was four and a half I recall reciting "The Night Before Christmas" at some function. I can remember loving that audience and I didn't have the slightest bit of stage fright. It was a large audience and I remember using a microphone and wearing a pink dress with long ribbons down the front and long curls (this was the Shirley Temple era). I must have been a terrible little exhibitionist. I would sing for anyone who asked and recite poetry at the drop of a hat. I always loved to be in plays in my grade school years, and I took a couple of years of drama in high school and one in college.

The only audiences that ever frightened me were the ones when I played the piano. This was particularly true when I played for a high school assembly. I would stand in the wings, and my hands would be all clammy and shaky, and I would think about all those kids out there that I knew (and I knew at least half a dozen who did not like me at all and would love to see me fall on my face), and I thought I could not go on. I did. After three measures, it was as if I were alone and I completely forgot my audience—I did not think about liking them or whether they liked me —they simply were no longer there.

For many years I took every emotion I had out on my piano. My mother never once had to ask me to practice but often had to ask me to quit. Even then (as now) I was prone to nocturnal communion with Rachmaninoff and Debussy. I imagine that my mother felt that the neighbors' music appreciation wore thin around midnight. My piano was my psychotherapist in those days, and as I told you, I turned to it again recently for the first time in ten years. I had almost forgotten how good it felt to play. It was, of course, frustrating at first after all those years. I had forgotten so much, and while my mind knew *exactly what to do, my fingers were not able to respond. But it has been the only activity which relieved the anxiety to any extent.*

Here was familiar ground that never changed. Surely Sibelius had experienced a wide range of emotions or he could never have written the "Romance" which runs the gamut from peaceful calm to thundering storm and back to calm again. I played the "Polonaise" again and thought about how Chopin could never have written it had he not suffered the loss of his home and seen Poland crushed. I nearly rememorized the "Polonaise" and halfway through memorizing it, I came to you last week. I have not played since. Now I type.

Dr. Odell began to add a little larger component of the hysteric to Helen's personality structure. He recounted to himself that the more usual hysterical woman is inclined to be dramatic, histrionic, to form short but intense relationships, to be "doers" rather than "thinkers." They have active fantasy lives, tend to exaggerate, and can be rather self-centered. The hysterical personality type often leans heavily on feminine charm and superficial manners, and often does love to exhibit herself. He made a mental note that Helen had leanings in this direction, but the hysterical diagnosis certainly didn't tell the whole story. Obviously she had been stable in her marriage, compulsive about her work, and was rather thoughtful and relevant in her conversation. This last part of her letter indicated that she had tried out the hysteric role and retreated from it.

He wondered what she was like after six drinks. He had the feeling if she were loosened up, she might still be willing to recite to an audience—perhaps not "The Night Before Christmas" but bawdy poems may be more likely.

When I was younger I used to have this idea that I was meant for "great things." I guess all of us have this feeling—it must be part of being human—when I am gone, I will leave something indelible to show that I have been here. I have an intense dislike of the ordinary. I have always wanted everything to be so special. For many years I labored under the delusion that during my lifetime I would paint a painting such as the world had never seen, or write the Great American Novel—or thrill the world with my music. Now I look at my hands, red from washing dishes with the nails short so I can type faster, and I really have to laugh. "These are the hands that were going to thrill the world."

Even as I write this, I think how nice it would be just to be ordinary and average and normal and satisfied with what I have, instead of some kind of nut feeling frightened out of my wits and running to see a headshrinker. Then I remind myself that I have a husband, a nice home, two extraordinary (mother's words) children, very good friends whom I have seriously neglected recently, a good job, and my physical health, and what else should anyone want? Then I am right back where I started.

It is hard for me to remember that only a few weeks ago I felt as if I really had life by the horns.

Nothing was impossible, I was convinced that one formed one's own destiny. I was not struggling with fears and invisible monsters which I did not understand. Oh, certainly I was worried about the dirty green paper with pictures of dead people on it—but so has everyone with a family and a mortgage and bills. But I felt that Steve and I had accomplished a great deal and we were well on Our Way. Since nothing essentially has changed in my life, I have to face the fact that something inside me has changed.

In this short time I have had my first good taste of insomnia, have had to see a therapist, and have never been so miserable in my life. I feel very much like a small metal pin with magnets all around it, so that it is pulled in every direction but goes no place. I have completely lost my sense of direction. My goal now is not to play Beethoven as it has never been played, nor to outdo Picasso, not to have the First Major Novel by a New Author reviewed by the New York papers. My goal is a restoration of tranquility —peace of mind—sanity, if you will.

Dr. Odell again felt a sharp twinge of antagonism towards Helen's mother. Helen's "great things" seemed to be another extension of her mother's denying her the ordinary everyday pleasures of being a woman. Helen had been bribed by her mother into not competing with her as a woman. By leading Helen into preparation for the life of a concert pianist, her mother had maintained control over the mundane household duties. Helen really had little choice but to settle for "great things."

I think I have digressed from family history as you requested it. I suppose you are interested in some aspects of my married life.

Since I truly grew up believing that I would never be married but would flit from one city to another giving concerts it is interesting that I married very young. I had always seen marriage as something you did because you couldn't do anything else. I have completely blocked my marriage ceremony out of memory. I vaguely remember smiling — keep it radiant, dear, you're the bride, remember? — and smiling and smiling until I thought my face would break. I do know, however, that I am legally wed because I have the photographs to prove it. Steve and I had rented an apartment and we stayed there on our wedding night and left the next morning for our honeymoon.

Ha! I'd sooner go on a week's bivouac with the Marines than go through that again. We were absolutely broke and would have starved to death if my mother hadn't packed us a lunch. Steve likes to tell the cute little story of his mature, enchanting bride in the Mother Hubbard flannel nightshirt sitting in bed crying because she missed her own room and her own bed—and her dog! We really should have gone to summer camp together and woven baskets. We were both twenty at the time. I can remember thinking on the way to Las Vegas, our little honeymoon spot, that life was over! I didn't really feel depressed exactly, just resigned. Now the white dress with the long train could be packed away where I would never have to look at it again. It was almost as if in getting married I had somehow failed. And she lived happily ever after and never played the piano again.

I am the only bride I ever knew whose husband came down with the chicken pox two weeks after the wedding. Tch, tch. And I had the colic.

I had never done laundry in my life. It seemed logical to me that when you got ready to wash clothes, you just washed clothes. You took everything you had that was dirty and you put it all in the washing machine and washed it. Blue jeans, white sheets, red towels, lingerie, they all went in together. None of them ever looked the same afterwards. Not having any better sense, I was not the least ashamed to hang it all on the line.

My honeymoon was the first time I had ever been away from home for as long as a week. We were both so immature I shudder now to think of us turned loose on a honeymoon trip. In addition to having a car that barely ran and nearly starving, we ran out of money altogether and I thought we were going to have to set up residence on the desert. Our lives have not changed much. We just do this now on a bigger scale. When we went to get the marriage license, Steve lacked a nickel of the required two dollars. The clerk chipped in five cents. I thought this was rather amusing at the time as I stood there in my levis, dirty sneakers, and Denver University sweatshirt, shuffling my feet and giggling, no doubt.

Two years ago Steve and I went on vacation to

Mexico. We bought every tourist item in sight and then found ourselves in Mexico City with twenty dollars in pesos. They have learned a great deal, our bride and groom. Our bride and groom cannot count. However, over the years we have become a bit more resourceful and managed to get back into the country without too much difficulty and without having to become Mexican citizens. And did this little experience bother our bride and groom? Not very much.

Dr. Odell reread the last couple of paragraphs to verify his sense of omission. He had been correct in his impression that nowhere was there reference to any fun, joy, warmth, or any pleasant emotion usually associated with a honeymoon. From experience he knew that the women who reported in that fashion were usually guilt ridden ones who could and did enjoy far more pleasure than they reported. It was not deliberate lying but an unconscious slanting and forgetting; in Helen's case she behaved as though her disapproving mother were constantly looking over her shoulder to make sure that she had no enjoyment and remained inadequate and dependent. Apparently Helen had been able to struggle successfully toward competency in her home and work which she was able to maintain until her mother visited her. He began to formulate a series of questions to put to her to test his theory that she had experienced a great deal of fun and joy early in her marriage.

I was just learning to respond to my married name when I discovered I was pregnant with Valerie. All during my pregnancy I ate lemons as if they were

the last grasp on life. With salt. I used to cut a lemon
and put it along with the salt shaker by the night-
stand before I went to sleep so it would be there when
I woke up in the morning. I also smoked like a fiend
(as I still do). I can remember once being down to
thirty cents and being torn as to whether to buy
lemons or cigarettes. I used to worry what the gar-
bage man would think about all those lemon peels,
and I would sort of hide them around among the many
cans I opened and the dumped-out cakes I ruined.

Steve was so nervous about Valerie's impending
birth that when the time came to go to the hospital,
he called my parents to go with us. My mother insisted
on being in the labor room with me. The next thought
is very interesting to me. While she was there, I felt
as if I did not dare make a sound. She hovered over
me and suffered every pain. I can remember biting my
lips so hard they bled, but I did not make a sound. I
did not show that it hurt. I wished the hell someone
would get her out of there. My father had left in great
haste at the first sniff of the sterile place. He was still
a bit shook because he had started to the hospital with
his pants on backwards. Steve sort of seemed to be in
and out of the room, but I think he was mostly relieved
that my parents were there to spell him. I finally did
whisper to the doctor to please get my mother out of
there before she had the baby for me. (I did not use
much bad language in those days as I do now, or it
would have been put in much stronger terms.) I still
did not yell, although I felt very much like heaping in-
vectives on the world in general and the tribulations

of womankind in particular—but I did not because I was afraid my mother was outside the door and would still hear me.

When Andy was born, here in Arizona, a good safe yelling distance from Denver, I yelled my head off. I threatened to put my foot in the doctor's face "if he did that once more," I complained bitterly about the heat, I vomited uninhibitedly, and I can remember making a deal with the doctor that if he could arrange for a boy this time, I would get this over before his lunch hour. I thoroughly enjoyed the whole experience. My mother wrote that she was "heartsick that she could not be with me and that I had to be so far away from home."

As he turned to the last page, Dr. Odell felt a twinge in his own stomach as he contemplated Helen's rejection of and discomfort in the woman's role. It was becoming more clear that Helen saw only two alternatives, both unpleasant. She could either remain a dependent child or she could assume her long-suffering mother's role. He hoped that in psychotherapy he could open her mind to other choices.

I can't think of any other information you asked for or anything I could add to this essay. As you can no doubt see, I have hardly had an eventful life. This whole autobiography seems so commonplace and average, I wonder now how I ever wrote so much. I have reread it and certainly find nothing to shed any light on my recent "scares." I almost feel as if I should have invented an early rape scene.

Anyway, make of it what you will. I have ac-

complished only one thing as far as I can see. Since I have written all this, I won't have to say it to you again.

Sincerely,
Helen James

The doctor thought that she would have to say it again many times.

Chapter 7

Dr. Odell put down Helen's history and reflected back on his own life. Her typewritten manuscript reminded him of his personal history—not so well written—he had prepared early in his training in clinical psychology. The writing of his own history had been part of a series of evaluative sessions and brief psychotherapy hours with Dr. Lenton, the chief of the clinical psychology training program. He winced a little as he remembered his own guarded, careful, overly scientific efforts to write a sufficiently detailed history to slide by without actually revealing anything of himself. He hadn't thought of any highly classified secrets he greatly needed to hide, but he had not trusted Dr. Lenton—at least not with the kind of trust necessary for telling of intimate happenings in his life or disclosing "forbidden" feelings.

He again shook his head in disbelief as he remembered how narrow and rigid other of his professors had been. For example, a graduate student's declaration of intent to go into private practice caused some professors to look at him with suspicion and belligerence and even to make vague threats about his "not graduating." He had not confided to Dr. Lenton that he planned to go into private practice, letting Dr. Lenton believe that he would be employed in a respectable mental health clinic or university-connected clinic with a strong research orientation.

Actually he had been so fed up with profound-sounding research, which was actually so much hot air, that he had not even picked up a scientific journal for three years after his doctoral graduation. He remembered well his professors' dreadful ambitions that psychology be as scientifically pure as physics, at the same time handing him a research book for study which contained descriptions of only ten psychological experiments on human beings to every five hundred on rats.

Actually, at the time, all he had learned from his therapy sessions with Dr. Lenton was that it was a very threatening, sometimes embarrassing, sometimes depressing position to be in—that of a patient across the desk from a therapist. He had never forgotten those painful, confused feelings of the initial hours of his own psychotherapy. He now tried to extend himself as a human person from the first meeting in the waiting room or the first minute in the office or the first moment a new patient talked to him on the telephone. He knew that he occasionally frightened away a patient who could not tolerate his warmth or intense attentiveness, since he couldn't "read" everyone correctly and give the new patient exactly the right amount of closeness or distance.

Perhaps he was a good therapist for Helen because he had once been almost as untrusting and as needy of closeness as she. His short-term psychotherapy in training and later his six years in a special brand of group therapy with other therapists had helped him feel much more trusting and affectionate, and much better able to discriminate whom he could trust and not trust.

He now knew he was permanently addicted to "relationships"—to a deeper involvement with other people, men, women, and children —who were open and real and wanted to give and receive the most personal thoughts and feelings others so seldom mentioned. He had felt a loneliness and a hunger for years before he could finally define exactly to himself that he needed and wanted more close relationships. And he knew now how to form these relationships.

He noted the time on his desk clock, but let himself have the luxury of a little more rumination.

Until he had become thirty years old, he had preferred to let friends and people he met believe he was a pampered son of an upper middle-class family of vague but adequate financial resources. He had been ashamed of being the second oldest child of a family of six children with farmer parents working on rented land. Six children seemed far too many for a dignified family, and a "rental farm" sounded like positively the worst level of living—too poor for respect and a little too good for real sympathy. One chance remark by a perceptive friend had started him thinking, and he had revised his estimate of himself, honestly feeling pride in getting his Ph.D. in an interesting new area of work.

He now felt far more open about his past and learned that his friends enjoyed hearing about "how it was" on a primitive 160 acre farm with no electricity and no plumbing. With his more reserved acquaintances he told about walking or riding a horse to a country school where all eight grades were in one room with a single teacher, or how in the summer he rode a horse all day long, from seven in the morning to six at night, to make one dollar for hauling water to a threshing crew.

To his closer friends he told stories about his early observations of the different shapes of penises on the farm animals and how different animals acted when mating and how he had felt about watching them, especially during his sex-obsessed adolescence. He related the fascination and repulsion he felt when he saw an old mother sow eat her own baby pigs. He told of his surprise and horror when he once idly kicked at the side of a dead cow and watched thousands of maggots spill out.

Only after his friends had reacted with unexpected respect had he realized his true accomplishment in singlehandedly managing his parents' farm during the summer he was fifteen. That summer both his father and older brother left the farm for better-paying jobs in war plants. He was left with full responsibility for planting and cultivating the crops, baling the hay, feeding the livestock, and repairing broken machinery—and a complete sense of inade-

quacy for achieving this adult assignment. His
brother, being the oldest, had been more fully trained
in running the farm while he, young Ross, had acquired his knowledge from watching his brother and
his father at work.

When he saw the two of them off at the train
station leaving for the war plant, he felt mad as hell
at his dad for leaving him with the farm—which he
mentally saw going down the drain as the train disappeared in the distance. When this dire prediction
was not fulfilled on the first day they were gone, nor
the day after that, Ross felt no pride or sense of
achievement, only relief that disaster had been averted
for one more day. Even at the end of the summer when
his brother and father returned and the farm showed
good crops and healthy animals, his family behaved
as if he had only done what was expected of him. His
was not a family for praise, and no one to this day had
ever commended him for his efforts or even so much
as mentioned them.

There were two major benefits to him from that
summer's experiences. He got out from under his
mother's thumb permanently; she never again had
any significant authority over him. Secondly, he ir-
revocably finalized his decision never to be a farmer.
He knew that never again did he intend to be tied to a
piece of land seven days a week, caring for the unending needs of animals twice a day, having no choice
about going out first thing in the morning and last
thing at night in blizzards, dust storms, or rain, and
using aching muscles and sore hands to be sure the

needs of the animals were met before his own could be thought of. There was just too damned much scooping, shoveling, carrying, pitching, turning, mowing, and monotonous unthinking activities.

A "higher education," always urged by his mother, became a quiet obsession. When he graduated from high school, he took a summer job to earn money for college. Once enrolled in the university, he continued working, sometimes holding down two jobs while going to school. During his first year he washed dishes at night in a sorority house and was an assistant at the university museum during the day when he had no classes. He now wondered where he had found the time for chasing girls and playing poker, both activities in which he had excelled and now remembered with a touch of nostalgia.

Dr. Odell became aware that in his reverie about his past—as in his present life—he tended to emphasize his accomplishments and virtues. He made himself deliberately dwell on his "bad" side. He hadn't always been so noble while growing up on the farm. He once built a small fire in the middle of a grain field, which got out of hand and would have destroyed the entire field had a neighbor not seen it and plowed a circle around the fire. He had seldom before or since been so terrorized and panicked. He had felt that his crime was visible from five miles up. His father had been away at the time, and Ross was physically ill by the time he got home, not even able to imagine what punishment his father would think of. Apparently Ross's attitude revealed his awareness of the calamity, for his father only scolded him gently for the incident.

Once his mother sent him to the store for thirty cents worth of meat. Ross had contrived the artful plan of buying twenty-seven cents worth of meat and spending three cents on candy, which he gobbled on the way home. His plan worked perfectly, but he suffered such guilt he had to confess to his mother. His career of thievery was short-lived.

He had been a little more capable in blackmail. He once caught his older brother, Ted, lighting a match in the barn which was full of dry hay, an act strictly forbidden by Father. After threats on Ross's part of telling about his brother's crime, he was able to force Ted to milk old Short Tits, the cow they all hated to milk because her teats were too small to grip so that it took twice as long to milk her as it did to milk any of their other cows. It was a totally unrewarding and dreaded chore. Two weeks later Ted reversed the strategy and vividly described to Ross how their father would treat a blackmailer, thus ending his brief taste of power over his older brother.

Mr. Odell, while shouldering the responsibility for raising six children during the Depression in an uncertain life on a rural farm, nevertheless arranged for his family to have fun. It was only many years later in his group therapy that Ross had realized that it was his father who would drive to town on Saturday afternoon and buy rodeo tickets for the family. It was his father who took a day off to make a snow plow in order that all the kids—including the neighbors—could get into town during the winter to go to the movies. It was Mr. Odell who regularly recharged the car batteries, which were used to operate the radio in the absence of electricity, so the Odell children could listen to "Jack Armstrong," "Orphan Annie," and "I Love a Mystery." On the isolated farm in the middle of winter, the radio was an important part of their lives.

Ross tended to accept his mother's values more than his father's. His mother repeatedly emphasized the importance of education, of being well dressed and using good manners, and of being "refined." She would have much preferred her husband to associate with bankers than sheepherders and failing in this aspiration, she transferred such ambitions to her children's lives. In this respect she was successful. Ross acquired his Ph.D. and his five brothers and sisters all completed college. His older brother became a lawyer, his younger brother was an architect, one sister became a nurse, and his younger sister a teacher. The youngest sister—and possibly the smartest— married almost the moment she received her liberal arts degree, and the marriage was happy and successful.

Until early in his own marriage, Ross had given most of the credit for the family's achievements to his mother, who actually did deserve credit for being intelligent, well read, and a true believer in education. In high school and college, Ross had felt ashamed of his father—and ashamed of his shame. His father had stubbornly persisted in wearing old-fashioned bib overalls, rolling his own cigarettes, and driving an ancient rattletrap pickup. He had often wondered how his mother could advocate such high standards of dress and "refinement," yet pick such a clodhopper for a husband. He still flinched when he remembered his father delivering him to high school in the rickety, dented pickup and his own desperate hope that no friends or enemies would see him emerge from such a disreputable vehicle.

It was during the first year of his marriage to Nora that Ross, while trying to describe the workings of his family to his new wife, surprised himself with his own changed perception of his father. In addition to recalling his father's providing most of the family fun, he began to put into perspective other memories of his father's traits. He told Nora of the time his dad, dressed in his typical hayseed costume, had gone to the monthly PTA meeting at the country school.

These monthly gatherings were eagerly awaited as the outstanding social event of each month, by both children and parents, for everyone in the family attended. During the business portion of the meeting the children played outside. Following the meeting, refreshments were served, the children joining the adults. Ross remembered the food was excellent, for the farm women were competitive and brought their finest delicacies. However, the ladies, becoming absorbed in conversation, nearly always burned the cocoa on the treacherous old kerosene stove in the corner of the schoolroom. He still associated the taste of burnt cocoa with those early PTA meetings.

On this particular evening the entertainment following the meeting was a ciphering contest, wherein two people at a time were given the same mathematical problem on the blackboard to see who could add the columns first, the winner remaining at the board. The first contestants were the older school children, who were quickly eliminated as the parents and teachers were drawn in. Mr. Odell had to be persuaded to come to the board and take part, Ross remembered, but he was the victor for the evening, even winning over the experienced school teacher and Ross's mother. Ross had felt both extremely proud and relieved, having seriously suspected that his mother was smarter. Ross had wanted a hero for a father.

Later, when Ross was in high school, his father never missed attending a school basketball game when Ross played. He would brave miserable road conditions and blizzard conditions to get the kids to important school functions. He would split his last dollar between Ross and Ted so they could go to the school dance. Ross had overlooked such talents as his father's ability to successfully repair farm equipment, to do all his own butchering, to be midwife to a variety of large and small farm animals, and to routinely accomplish a dozen other tasks that would frighten and baffle the specialized man of today.

Ross could keep his mind more open today when he simply reminded himself of his own biased viewpoint as he was growing up. In terms of his competitiveness with his father for his mother's affections he had been convinced that his father was not ambitious, that he was narrow-minded, and that he had no true consideration for his family. He was now able to perceive that his father truly was a kindly, generous, intelligent man who had his own problems but was more of a man and a human than the more prosperous fathers that Ross had envied.

Then there were women. For various healthy and unhealthy reasons, adolescent Ross, young man Ross, and middle-aged Ross had all shared the same basic attitude toward women. He enjoyed females in a variety of ways—looking at them, talking to them, sometimes arguing with them, and working with them. He usually managed to have lunch with one of the social workers or secretaries—or both—a couple of days a week. Various of his colleagues had rather openly speculated as to whether he was a chaser, really preferring to believe that he was. It was quite inconceivable to them that a man and woman could work closely together, talk together, or spend time together without becoming sexually involved. When Ross's wife would join him and his secretary for lunch, it only seemed to pique their curiosity. Ross freely admitted to feelings of sexual attraction and affection toward half a dozen women but persistently disproved his colleagues who predicted either an affair or a state of intolerable frustration. As the years went by and neither of these events occurred while Ross continued his luncheon dates and friendships with women, his colleagues' attitudes remained somewhere between envy and disbelief.

Ross had been concerned about their opinions until he began to realize that many men really do not like women and have difficulty accepting them in roles other than being a mother or sexual object. That a woman could be a friend and companion was totally unfamiliar to them. Despite Ross's own use of and belief in psychoanalytic theory, he was now convinced that psychoanalytic training and a personal psychoanalysis did not necessarily overcome a deep-seated mistrust of women.

Ross had married his college sweetheart. Nora Odell often gave people the first impression of being shy, reserved, and uncommunicative. She was tiny and delicate looking, and once had been asked if she moved to Arizona for her health. The truth was she was never sick and rarely tired. She had quietly and effectively worked as a secretary to help support Ross through five years of doctoral training in psychology. She ran her household with a minimum of fuss and a maximum of efficiency. She never seemed pressured for time and was a welcome relief to Ross who was accustomed to direct and indirect demands on his time and emotions every day.

Except when he and Nora were having one of their more quiet kinds of conflicts, the best part of his day was starting as he pulled into his own driveway in the evening. After nineteen years of marriage he still felt warmed when he saw Nora's slender figure moving casually about the kitchen as he came in the back door. Sometimes he wished she were more obviously glamorous or dramatic, but he always had second thoughts and realized he had made a wise choice. Although inclined to be stubborn and with-holding, she kept improving every year toward being a warmer and more open person.

Ross reflected on the absence of any sexual ma-terial in Helen's history. This omission did not sur-prise him. He remembered his own fumbling and em-barrassed efforts to meet the demands of the section entitled "Sexual History" for Dr. Lenton. He tried to steer a middle course somewhere between appearing as a sex fiend, a eunuch, or worst of all, homosexual. Each question was answered not so much with an ef-fort toward honesty but with the idea of sounding as sexually "normal" as possible. In addition he had the terrible fear that a copy would fall into his recent bride's hands. Even then he didn't know whether she would be horrified by his many exploits or ashamed of his lack of experience. One question Dr. Lenton had asked him during the psychotherapy sessions was, "Have you ever worried about the length of your penis?" Ross had been initially shocked since so per-sonal and direct a question had never been put to him before. He had become flustered and groped for words and finally responded, "Well, yes, I guess I have." Dr. Lenton's knowing smile and remark, "What man hasn't?" had eased the tension.

Dr. Lenton had merely glanced at Ross's com-ments about masturbation and had not been impres-sed by a half a dozen short-lived sexual episodes with girls. Ross had omitted any reference to some sex play with his younger sister in grade school. At the time

Ross felt that such an admission was too shameful and perverse to share with anyone. He had been fairly easily able to disclose the facts surrounding several homosexual advances that had been made towards him in college and in the service, for he felt that these advances reflected no guilt on his part. He wasn't sure whether Dr. Lenton was envious or dubious when he talked about having had sexual relations with his first serious girl five times in two hours. Now at his present age, Ross was pretty sure Dr. Lenton had had both reactions.

Ross hoped he had educated his children about sexuality not only factually but emotionally so that they would find their teen-age years less anxious and disturbing than he had. He held no particular grudge against his parents who had not been verbal or directly instructive in sexual matters because they had unconsciously served as good models of affection and sexual behavior.

Ross liked being a father. He often worried that he didn't spend enough time with his two children, but knew that they shared a deep attachment. Ross knew he was inclined to be an old-fashioned father with an emphasis on firmness and adherence to the family rules. He had standing arguments and real differences with several colleagues who promoted permissiveness and were overindulgent towards their children. He encouraged his children to discuss their feelings, partly by being frank about his own feelings and partly by exerting continual gentle pressure to alert them to their own emotions. He did get angry and loud on numerous occasions. He apologized when he felt he was in the wrong. He did give them full attention when he spent time with them. He worried about his son and knew he put more pressure on him than his daughter, feeling a responsibility to help his son in the male role. Sometimes he felt he was able to enjoy his daughter more since his wife took a greater responsibility for her training and development.

His thoughts about his children reminded him of Helen's only enthusiastic positive statement in her first hour, that about her children. Like himself, she seemed to enjoy being a parent and her children made her happy. In fact, from her answers in their interview, he guessed that it was more natural and spontaneous for her to express warmth and approval than it was for him. Her parents must have given her a substantial amount of love and affection or she would not have been able to be so expressive with her children. Thinking in terms of Helen's present low self-esteem, he wondered what had gone wrong.

He wondered which was worse: Helen's parents' demonstrative show of affection mixed with disguised anger or his own parents' sparsity of direct approval and more open aggressiveness.

He decided he would not have traded parents.

CHAPTER 8

By the time Helen arrived for her next appointment following Dr. Odell's receipt of her written history, he had convinced himself that they had a better relationship than actually existed. Her openness in writing about herself persuaded him that he knew her well. He felt equipped to dig right into therapy with her. In his enthusiasm, he forgot to take into account that she had not been privy to any such private history about him, and therefore he was still as much a stranger to her as before.

She matched his warmth when he greeted her in the waiting room, but once he closed the door of his office behind them he realized the warmth had been only conventional politeness. Once alone with him, she was obviously uncomfortable. She sat down in her chair hesitantly, eyed the door, launched into a nervous monologue about the weather, the traffic, and her concern about the right front tire of her car. She was holding him at arm's length and delaying as long as possible any mention of her reason for being there.

Dr. Odell allowed her several moments to adjust to his presence before he interrupted her. "I received your history and enjoyed reading it."

"Was it too long?" she asked, too quickly. (You're damn right it was too long. I practically poured out every feeling I have had from the crib to present. I wish the hell I had made a carbon copy so I could remember all I told him. Whatever it was, it was too much. I shouldn't have written it when I felt so lonely. I wrote it as if no one but I would ever read it.)

"No, not for me. I'm a reader and I've learned a lonely. I wrote it as if no one but I would ever read it.)

"No, not for me. I'm a reader and I've learned a lot from reading. I was a bit surprised at the work and effort you put into it.

"I surprised myself in that regard. I wished after I mailed it that I had edited it. In fact, I feel as if I have told you everything about myself that there is to tell." (Everything except that I feel no better, Dr. Odell. I know no more about myself or what is troubling me than I did that first day in my office. And I had two "scares" this week. Two dillies. But I don't know how to tell you about them any better than I did last week.)

"Maybe you scared yourself—like telling me too much too fast," he suggested. "It's not wise to rush into too many secrets. Don't push too hard." Privately he remembered her quick withdrawal into silence in their first hour when she felt she had revealed too much of herself.

"I know that's my trouble today," Helen said.

"I have had absolute nightmares about sending those many pages to you. I was sorry the minute I mailed the history. If I could have got it back out of the mailbox I would have."

"Well, I've already read it, so I can't undo that. Now that it's done, let's get the most out of it that we can. For one thing, we have learned that you tend to get in a little too deep and then back out and worry about it." Damn, he thought to himself. She is sensitive. I'm going to have to be careful about inviting confidences that she'll regret and worry about the rest of the week. Go slowly, Ross.

"You're right. It sounds familiar. Blab now, pay later, that's me." (Seems as if I should have learned that from past painful experiences.)

"Remember, between what goes on in my own head and what patients have told me, it's pretty hard to shock me. From your history I can't remember any shocking event, but I did like the way you can show your feelings in writing."

"I told you I was very ordinary. It was not my intent to shock you."

Thus it went for the rest of the session, a verbal sparring in which little was gained. If he supported or approved, she twisted his statement to an implied criticism. If he questioned, she became defensive or silent. When in desperation he referred to some sentences from her written history, she all but denied its authorship. Nonetheless she made another appointment for the next week.

Using this tiny display of confidence in him, after

he wrote her name in his appointment book, he broached the idea with her of doing psychological testing. He quickly reasoned to himself that the more structured "question and answer" situation might permit her to relax and to become acquainted with him in an indirect way. His second reason was the mild but persistent fear that he had underestimated the severity and immediacy of her problems, in which case the psychological tests would confirm or deny his initial appraisal.

The following several sessions he administered the battery of psychological tests plus giving her several "homework" tests. In the test situation, it was hard to recognize Helen as the same reticent, defensive, threatened woman she had been in her two short therapy hours. She was comfortable, interested, often enthusiastic and appeared to enjoy intellectual competitiveness. Dr. Odell laughed with her as her sense of humor emerged, not in the brittle and masochistic way it had in the first two sessions, but in a healthy and spontaneous exchange with the doctor. Helen particularly enjoyed the Rorschach test, the ink blot test, but refused to take it too seriously. There were too many cartoons about it. She gave legitimate responses to each test card, but couldn't resist adding comical comments to each one. Dr. Odell believed he had been correct in giving the tests. By doing so he had confirmed her basic strength, and he sensed the definite beginning of friendship.

On the day she came in to hear the results of her tests, things went very well until the final few min-

utes. They discussed the test findings with a continuing sense of camaraderie.

"Basically what I am saying," Dr. Odell said at
the conclusion of the hour, "is that you're a sane and
intelligent woman with a lot of warmth and strength,
but your problem right now is that for unexplained
reasons you get to feeling anxious, guilty, and depressed. Your mind has hidden the real reasons, and
we need to work together to unearth these seeming
monsters."

"You make us sound like detectives," Helen said
smiling. "I'm a great fan of Ellery Queen. Also I'd
much rather feel like a detective than a mental patient.
Stealthily seeking out the dirty villain in my gray
matter—that's how I'll think of this procedure." (I'm
beginning to like him. Maybe the two of us can defeat
my "scares.")

"It is a joint venture," he said, "and it will take
both of us working together to combat the hidden
side of you that is giving you the pain. Your particular
weakness probably shows up on the job as well as in
your family and private life. You may get some side
benefits at the office as well as at home."

Helen stiffened. "I suppose that's possible," she
said, tightlipped. (Weakness! Who ever said I was
weak! He just said I had strength. And I do. No matter how bad I had felt these last few weeks, I haven't
neglected my duties. Particularly at the office! How
dare he insinuate that my weakness shows up on the
job. I don't need any side benefits at work. I'm beginning to think I've made a big thing over a small case

of nerves. Just when I was beginning to trust him. Hell with him.)

Dr. Odell saw her stiffen and wondered what had happened. He quickly reviewed his last few statements to her and couldn't understand her change into the now familiar formal tone of voice and rigid pose. Perhaps he was over reading her reaction. She might not be responding to him at all.

"I see our time is up for today," he said, wishing he had more time to explore her change in attitude. "Is there any last question you have?"

"No."

"Is this same time all right next week?"

"Yes, it's fine." (Anything is fine if I can get out of here. He has no more idea of what's troubling me than I do. Instead of helping me, he attacks me. I'll never come back.)

"Good. I'll see you next week," Dr. Odell said, as he walked her to the door.

The next day Dr. Odell's secretary informed him that she had received a call from Mrs. James cancelling her next appointment. She had left no explanation.

Dr. Odell thought back to their session the day before. He remembered her distant behavior at the end of the hour, but still could not think of a reason for it. He considered calling her when he received the message but decided to wait a few days, hoping she had merely discovered she had a conflicting appointment or that an out-of-town trip had come up. In the back of his mind, he was sure this wasn't true. He felt he knew her well enough now to guess he had frightened her off; he just had no idea how he had done it. He hoped that by waiting she would think it over and call on her own initiative. She didn't however.

He waited until the day of her canceled appointment and then called Helen at her office. Her voice was brisk and businesslike as she informed him she would not be returning to see him again.

"I don't understand," Dr. Odell said. "Would you please tell me what has happened. This sudden break frankly has me confused."

"Nothing has happened," she answered impersonally. He wondered if someone were standing near her so she couldn't speak freely, or if she were simply trying to get rid of him. "I have decided we have a personality conflict. I still intend to continue treatment. I have made an appointment with someone else."

"I certainly recognize that this is your choice," Dr. Odell answered, "but it's possible you're being overly sensitive or you may have taken offense to something I've said unintentionally." Privately he thought her excuse about a "personality conflict" was unfair. It was somehow like telling him he "had a bad aura," an undefined criticism that can't be changed or apologized for. She was obviously angry with him but unwilling to deal with her anger directly and choosing instead to hold a grudge and to terminate the relationship on a basis justifiable to her.

He left a time interval for her to respond. When

she didn't he thought to himself: Take a chance. Set an example, even if it's a bad one. Tell her off a little.

"Damn it, you make me angry," he said. "Everything seemed fine at the end of our last hour, and now all of a sudden you are cold and bitchy and unreasonable. You're willing to forget me forever rather than tell me what you're annoyed about."

There was a stunned silence before she answered. "I'm sorry you're angry at me," she said, and her voice warmed somewhat, "but I really cannot come back." Her voice became cool again as she added. "I have already sent you an authorization to forward the results of my tests to my new doctor. Good-by." She hung up, breaking the connection before he could respond.

A few days later he received a note from Irv Steinberg saying that Mrs. Helen James was a new patient of his. He requested that Dr. Odell forward his results of psychological testing. Enclosed was Helen's signed authorization. With regret, Dr. Odell forwarded the report to Dr. Steinberg. It was the twentieth of October.

November came and went. The days were now balmy, and tourists began to arrive for the Phoenix winter season. Local residents had planted winter lawns which were now green, and in the citrus areas of the city the fruit was beginning to ripen for harvest in December. Social life picked up in Phoenix after the long hot summer. The symphony season began, golf courses became busy and it was hard to get a tee time, and college football was in full swing. Dr. Odell was busy in his practice and in his social life.

Occasionally he was reminded of Helen James and wondered what had happened to her. Her sudden and unexplained departure nagged at him sufficiently for him to bring up her case with the countertransference group of therapists.

He described to the group not only Helen's history and problems, but his own feelings and reactions to her. He told of her first anxiety attack following an argument with her husband and her inability to confide in her family doctor, her family, or her friends. He described her brittle and defensive attitude in their first two sessions, in sharp contrast to the warmth she had displayed in her writing of her history. He reported her sporadic periods of warmth and humor, sometimes followed by a withdrawal into frozen aloofness at the slightest provocation.

He told the group of his initial apprehension when he heard her depressed-sounding voice on the phone the first time followed by his relief when he saw her in the waiting room looking well dressed and composed. He admitted his immediate male interest in her, describing her to the group as "a well-stacked, feminine, alert woman." He described the vicissitudes of their on-and-off relationship and his bafflement at her aloof departure at the end of an hour in which he felt rapport had been established. He ended by relating her telephone cancellation of her next appointment and his subsequent call to her in which he expressed his anger at her cool dismissal.

In short order his fellow therapists convinced him that he was simply continuing his familiar pattern, that of emotionally moving in on people too rapidly. They cited earlier examples in which he had frightened away patients whom he particularly liked and wanted to work with. His confronting friend, Jeff, summarized the problem when he said, "You're too damned intimate and chummy before the patient has a chance to know you and to know what you really mean by it."

Ross countered by pointing out his knowledge of this facet of himself and how carefully he had tried to avoid this problem with Helen by cautiously choosing his words and phrasing. The group won the argument, however, by reminding him that it was not only his wording or phrasing that threatened the patient; it was his tone of voice, his facial expression—his entire manner which conveyed an overeager attitude. Ross left the meeting feeling chastised but philosophical. He did not tell the group that night that he still stubbornly believed that he would rather err on the side of warm openness than on the side of cold intellect.

It was Dr. Odell's custom to let his secretary take an extra hour at lunchtime for Christmas shopping during December. His fellow doctors frowned on his permissiveness, grumbling to him that it set a bad example for the other girls in the building. Dr. Odell continued his tradition, despite his colleagues' protests, because his secretary genuinely appreciated this privilege and more than made up for it by uncomplainingly offering to stay late to get an urgent report typed and cheerfully helping make up for his deficiencies. She had long ago philosophically accepted the fact that he procrastinated in his dictation until the last deadline was imminent and she unvaryingly typed and mailed them the same day. Thus he answered his own phone during the extra hour she was gone Christmas shopping.

It was during one of these hours that Helen James called.

"You startled me, Helen. I didn't expect you to be on the phone," he said. "I'm glad to hear your voice. I've thought about you often." Damn it, I'm doing it again, he thought. I'm treating her like a friend when I know she can't tolerate that status. I've got to remember to be more formal and professional.

"I'm glad to hear your voice, too," Helen said, with genuine pleasure. "In fact, you'll never know how glad. If you can stand another go at therapy with me, I'd like to come back and see you."

"I see," he answered in his best professional manner. "You need a late afternoon appointment, don't you, Mrs. James because of your job?"

"Yes, the same time as I had before if you can work it out," she said.

"I believe that the five o'clock hour on next Tuesday is available if you would like it." He felt he was successfully avoiding the familiarity and eagerness his colleagues had warned him about. She accepted the appointment and Dr. Odell vowed he would handle her next hour with professional aplomb.

The following Tuesday at five o'clock Dr. Odell

greeted Helen in the waiting room. Once again she was friendly and smiling, but he doubted that her demeanor would survive once they were alone in his office. He remembered Jeff's admonition and consciously tried to appear somewhere between interested and detached.

Helen's conviviality persisted and she plumped herself into her chair, relaxed, and lit a cigarette. Jauntily tossing her match into the ashtray, she smiled and asked, "What's your favorite color?"

"Uhhhh—blue," Dr. Odell responded, a little taken aback.

"Do you like music?" A mischievous smile playing about her mouth.

"Yes, most of it," he answered, truly puzzled now, but determined to continue his role of the dignified therapist.

"Where did you grow up?" This time she barely stifled a giggle.

"Nebraska—on a farm," he answered. He could no longer maintain his uninvolved air. "Damn it, I told you that already. I know you don't suffer from loss of memory. Let me in on the game you are enjoying so much."

"Now, that's more like the Dr. Odell I remember. In case you're interested, you just passed a test."

"I've heard of Twenty Questions, but never the Three-Question Test. It doesn't seem to me you have to be very bright to pass that test."

"Oh, but it's not brightness that counts. It's a test for honesty. Would you believe there are some learned people who won't answer those three questions?"

"Helen, I'm a patient man but I'm thinking about hitting you. Explain."

"Since I last saw you, I have had an experience I can't believe. I was mad as hell at you when I left that last day. You made a remark about my weakness that really hit an exposed nerve. I concluded that you were picking on me and attacking me by merely mentioning the possibility I had a weakness, especially since I was beginning to feel you were my friend. I decided I would find a new therapist who was more understanding of my true strong nature." Again her dimples deepened and Dr. Odell realized she was making fun of herself.

"You do get so touchy and sensitive that I feel as though I have to be very careful this very minute or you'll run out on me again. How was I to know the word 'weakness' would insult you?"

"I learned recently that there is a lot to be said for frankness, even if it isn't always pleasant. You've got me off the track. I want to explain the three questions."

"I wish you would. I'm curious," he answered.

"As you know, I fled from you and went to see Dr. Steinberg. I saw him twice. I only went back the second time because I couldn't believe what happened the first time. Do you know that man never answered one of my questions? He only responded with another question. I asked him what I thought were perfectly legitimate things about my 'scares,' and his response was evasiveness. The second time I went back to him I decided I would try those same three innocent questions I just asked you. Would you care to hear his answers?"

"Yes, I would. I'd never thought of him as being that different from me. I've talked to him at a half a dozen parties and he seems pleasant enough."

"Maybe at a party. Try being his patient once."

"Be specific. So far you have only tantalized me."

He was wondering to himself what she meant. He knew Irving Steinberg socially, although he wasn't a close friend, and had always found him to be reasonable and affable, though perhaps a bit staid. He hadn't been impressed by Irving's warmth, openness, or wittiness, but he had never found him objectionable. He was a person that others neither avoided nor sought out.

"At least you have a reaction. And you didn't answer me with a question. So as your reward I will give you specifics. The first hour I spent with that man I was so uncomfortable and nervous I could barely speak. He did nothing to put me at ease. Perhaps this is a form of treatment—I don't know. I described my 'scares' and feelings to him as best I could, and the only way I knew he was still alive was that he tugged at his beard. When I left he hadn't said one meaningful sentence to me. Oh, yes—he did. Once when I in desperation asked him if he had ever had crazy thoughts, he answered, 'We are not concerned in here with my thoughts, only yours.' Well, it simply gave me the feeling that by admitting I had thoughts at all was admitting lunacy."

"Come on, now, aren't you being a bit hard on him?" Dr. Odell asked. He thought to himself that Irving talked too little and he himself talked too much.

"That is exactly what I thought. That's the reason I went back the second time. I was certain it was my fault in some way. When I'm really uptight as I was with him, I am sure I could even upset Freud."

"I hate to admit it, but I'm feeling very flattered," Dr. Odell said.

"You have just admitted a feeling. Two points in your favor. Also you answered all three of my contrived questions. Just listen to the answers Steinberg gave me to them. I decided in the second hour I'd ask him some simple innocent questions and see if he would answer me. When I asked him his favorite color, he looked a bit startled and said, 'What do you think my favorite color would be?' I told him I had no idea and he asked me what my favorite color was. I told him I wasn't sure—which was a lie—but I knew that if I said 'blue' he would say I was depressed, or if I said 'green' he would diagnose me as envious. When I asked him if he liked music he asked, 'What kind of music?' 'Any kind of music,' I said. He told me it was far too general a question to answer and that I was trying to avoid answering his questions. This puzzled me because he hadn't asked me any questions, just stared at me and stroked his beard. I finally volunteered that I had grown up in Colorado and asked him where he was raised. 'Why do you ask?' he responded. "I felt as if I had intruded on his privacy in some unforgiveable way. I left his office hoping he would go home and ask his wife what she was preparing for dinner and she would answer, 'What do you think we are having for dinner?' Do they behave that way with their friends and families, too, or is it some special technique for making patients feel ridiculous?"

"I'm certain his intent was not to make you feel ridiculous. You know, you have just described a typical psychoanalyst, but you make him sound so dreadful. You must have a particular sensitivity that causes you to reject his approach so strongly."

"Well, I sure as hell can't sit for an hour and talk to someone who doesn't respond at all. It seems rather inhuman to me—it doesn't work in any other situation in life."

"Therapy is a special situation which is not like any other in life," he answered.

"I can't really believe it is that different. It is unnatural to put two adults in a room and ask one to do all the talking. Also I notice that you don't do that. I wouldn't be back here again if you did." (Not that I'm glad I'm back. He seems to be defending Steinberg against me.)

"I'm not sure if you have come back because of my sinfulness or my virtues," he said. Dr. Odell felt that the psychoanalytic theory of "silence" to provoke anxiety in the patient and therefore stimulate relevant verbalizations to relieve the anxiety was a worthwhile theory. The same technique could be used, however, for the therapist to hide himself and yet place a disproportionate burden of guilty resistance on the patient. It sounded as if this was what had happened with Helen and Steinberg.

"Your sinfulness, of course," she answered immediately. "If talking and communicating are 'sinful' in this situation, I want no part of virtue. I have one uncommunicative, silent man at home and have no room in my life for any more saints."

"I hate to bring up such an unpopular subject as psychotherapy, but could you fill me in a little bit on your 'saint' at home."

"Okay. If we really have to stop playing, I will get down to the nitty-gritty," she said. (I wish I knew what the nitty-gritty was. So far I feel that my second hour with Steinberg has cost me another hour's fee in here.) "I was just wondering why I had referred to my husband as a saint. I think it's because he puts himself in a position where he assumes no responsibility and yet can sit back and judge everyone else's behavior. Because that is what Steve has done. Over the past fifteen years of our marriage I have gradually assumed all the responsibility in our relationship. I don't like it, but I don't know how to get out of it. When you have to make all the decisions, you are bound to make a few bloopers, and the ax falls when I do. Do you know what he accused me of a few months ago?"

"What?"

"He actually accused me of jeopardizing our financial future because I had made no investments.

Do you know any other wife who has been accused of this particular crime? I know I couldn't have been put in this position if I had not handled all the budgeting and bill paying all these years. Yet I am afraid to turn the checkbook over to him."

"Why?"

"Because the damned fool would buy an airplane. We have been having a running battle for three months about his going in with some buddy of his for half share of a $9,000 airplane. Each time I win the argument against the plane, he makes me feel if only I would relent, it would be the beginning of our fortune. I know it isn't true, but it keeps me feeling as if he is right and I am wrong."

"You mentioned the argument over the airplane the first day you came in. Wasn't that the night before you had your first anxiety attack? Has that become a repetitive battle?"

"It has and it hasn't. It's become repetitive in the sense that it comes up over and over again. But the strange part of it is that I don't think Steve really wants that plane now. I think he wants to use the plane as a club to beat me over the head with whenever we argue about something else," she said, as if the thought had only occurred to her just now. "For instance, we have argued about the money for my therapy. Having to admit that I need help is bad enough. It's doubly painful when he makes me feel that by spending money on therapy I am depriving us of a financial future. He doesn't really come out and say it but he subtly implies that therapy is a self-indulgent luxury which is depriving the entire family from financial security."

"Your husband sounds as if he is a guilt manipulator," Dr. Odell said. "In other words, he knows what makes you feel guilty, and he brings it up at the right time and the right place to get what he wants from you."

"Except that he usually doesn't get it. I mean I didn't give in to his wishes about the plane, and here I am using up sixty cents a minute of our family's future against his wishes, so while I may in fact feel guilty—and I must admit that I do—he hasn't actually got what he wants. It seems we both lose."

"Maybe if he doesn't get what he wants from you, the next best thing is to make you miserable—like punishing you for not gratifying his wishes."

"Do you mean he does this intentionally?" Helen asked. (If that son-of-a-bitch is purposely driving me out of my mind, I have a different problem than I thought. If Steve wants a misery contest, I'll give him one.)

"I don't know whether it's intentional or not because I don't know your husband. It is doubtful that it is, but in any event, it has the same effect on you either way. Maybe it would help sometime if I could see your husband and get to know him a little bit." He thought to himself that it would be useful to him to see Helen's husband. It was often too easy to take sides wholeheartedly with the spouse he was seeing regularly and join in blaming the mate at home.

"He'd never come in. He thinks this sort of thing

is silly and a waste of time," Helen told him. "Besides he is quite happy and comfortable with the situation as is. If I felt as well as he does I wouldn't want to come in either."

"If he won't come in for himself or because he feels a portion of blame for your marital problems, do you think he would come in just to please you?"

"You must be kidding. You are misjudging his desire to please me, Doctor. I'll ask him, but I don't hold out much hope. However, it is the Christmas season so maybe he will be full of good cheer." She sat quietly for a moment and then continued. "Let me tell you what happened the other night. It will give you an idea of his wish to make me happy. He came home from the office after a few Yuletide drinks with the boys and invited me to go get a tree with him.

"Happily I agreed and we took the kids and went to the Christmas tree lot and chose a tree. When the man had put a stand on it and told us the price was ten dollars, Steve waited for me to pay for it. Ordinarily I would have done so and argued it out with him at home that he had invited me and I assumed he had the money for the tree. I couldn't do this, however, because I hadn't brought along my purse. Steve reluctantly paid for the tree, and when we were in the car driving home he angrily informed me that I owed him ten dollars for the tree. The children were with us so I choked back my own anger until we were home.

"All the way home I furiously thought of all the things I would say to him about being the provider and being stingy and always depending on me to be along to pay for anything we bought. Then I remembered that it was Christmas and I couldn't stand the thought of a fight which would end with his stomping out of the house, so I silently paid him the ten dollars when we got home and tried to forget about it."

"I see you still have a lot of feelings about it, so I guess you weren't able to forget it."

"Obviously not or I wouldn't be telling you about it now and bawling," she said, blowing her nose on the Kleenex he had offered to her. "When it comes to Christmas trees, I don't have the best of luck in the world.

"When I was a little girl, my parents had practically no money. It was at the end of the Depression and I sometimes wonder how they did as well as they did. The Christmas when I was four or five, I was happily anticipating a huge tree which could touch the ceiling. Before we went to choose a tree my mother told me a little story. She told me about the Christmas tree lot where they had lots of tall, bushy, beautiful trees and one tiny scraggly little tree in the corner. As all the people came to pick their tree, no one even glanced at the pitiful little one standing off by itself to one side. One by one all the big trees were sold and on Christmas Eve the little tree with so few branches still stood on the lot, now all alone. It was very sad as it had wanted so much to be decorated and be in someone's house on Christmas morning.

"Immediately at the end of the story we would leave for the tree lot. Need I tell you which tree we brought home? I would scour the lot for the tiniest, scrawniest tree they had. Of course it was always the cheapest, too. At least as a child I didn't have to pay them back for the tree on the way home." She attempted a weak laugh, but there was bitterness in her tone. Dr. Odell did not know whether it was directed at her parents or at Steve.

"How do you feel towards your mother now when you think about this Christmas tree story?" he asked her. My God, he thought, does she realize what she is telling me about her mother?

"Towards my mother?" Helen asked, looking perplexed. "I thought she chose a very clever way of getting me to choose a tree that they could afford. How did my mother get into this? I thought we were going to discuss Steve's stingy, selfish, Scrooge maneuvers."

"Yes, you're right. We'll return to your mother later." He realized he had just about put his foot in his mouth and brought up something Helen couldn't handle. As she had told the story, he felt she was more aware than she actually was of her mother's managing tactics and her own feelings about how her mother operated. Now he realized the bitterness was aimed at Steve alone at the conscious level. He thought how easy it had been for Helen's mother to justify this method of raising her daughter, but the plain truth was that her mother had capitalized on Helen's sympathetic feelings and trained her to choose the least desirable and, even worse, to prefer the undesirable. He began to wonder if she applied this same rule to other areas of her life.

He glanced at his desk clock. "I see it's about that time," he said. "I would like to see your husband, but only when you feel comfortable about it."

"It's not I who am uncomfortable about it," she said. "I think it's a good idea. I have the feeling that I'm too hard on him sometimes, and I'd like to get your viewpoint. I must admit the idea makes me a little nervous though. Steve has such a logical, sensible way of putting things, I suppose I'm a little afraid he'll win you over to his side. I have the feeling Steve is a man's man. Men always seem to like him, and I guess I am a little reluctant even to take a chance that you two will get together and become buddies and agree that his wife is a kook."

"Why don't you talk it over with him, but we won't set any definite date until you and I have discussed it further." He sensed that her reluctance was great enough he didn't wish to press the point further for the time being. She did not yet trust him sufficiently.

"Agreed," she said, smiling.

As she left his office, Dr. Odell felt convinced that she would return.

CHAPTER 9

Helen was ten minutes late for her next visit and was breathless as she rushed in. Her tardiness was habitual and varied from two to fifteen minutes each time. The first few visits that this occurred Dr. Odell thought maybe she wasn't going to show up at all. He was now becoming accustomed to her late and precipitous entrances and was considering how to deal with them when she arrived this day.

"It's not my fault I'm late." Her words spilled over one another as she said, "It's the City of Phoenix who is conspiring for me not to get here. Have you ever timed that traffic light on the corner? The one where I have to make a left hand turn onto this street? Well, it's green for about three seconds and red for at least thirty minutes. My God. I don't know why I arrange this appointment during the five o'clock traffic." She dropped into her chair as if exhausted, whether from her trip across town or her speech he wasn't certain.

He wondered for the dozenth time why she was

late and continued to be late each time. He had called it to her attention, scolded her gently, and thrown the subject open for discussion several times, all to no avail.

"You are so efficient in most ways and so dollar conscious that it really puzzles me as to how you can waste one fifth of your hour."

"It's my money, and I'm fully aware it has just cost me six dollars today. Really—I am working on it and trying to be more punctual. It drives Steve crazy, too—my tardiness. Let's not talk about it today. I have something else I want to tell you about."

Helen announced that she had considered the idea of Steve's coming in to see Dr. Odell, that she had discussed it with Steve, and that he had agreed.

"He wasn't exactly overjoyed at the idea, I might add," she said. "I had to threaten him a little. His first response was that he could see no possible way his coming to see a headshrinker would help me. Knowing him as I do I accused him of being chicken. I was pretty sure he couldn't stand the thought that I could endure something that he couldn't. So finally he said he would come 'for me.' Actually he is only going to do it to prove he isn't cowardly."

"I'm glad he's coming in," Dr. Odell said. "Are you sure you haven't exaggerated his lack of concern? It's pretty hard to read somebody else's motives that well."

Helen assumed her pseudocute, coy manner and said, "Exaggerate! Me! Why, Doctor, how could you think such a thing?"

"I have hinted that you're not given to under-statements," he said, chuckling. Her responsive smile encouraged him to continue. "Seriously, I want you to remember that you should take everything he says after the session with a grain of salt. Particularly if he is annoyed or angry about coming in, he might take an innocent phrase of mine and hit you over the head with it."

"You mean something like my taking your inno-cent phrases and interpreting them as attacks on my abilities?" she answered. "I think you are still re-membering my escape to Steinberg when you men-tioned the possibility I had a weakness."

"Right. You know how easy it is to do now," he said. "Remember; don't judge me in terms of any-thing your husband might say."

"If you warn me one more time, I will be con-vinced that you have a dark secret plan to form a con-spiracy with him," Helen answered. (What in hell does he have in mind discussing with Steve anyway? I'm beginning to wonder if I even want the two of them to meet.) She decided to come out in the open with her private thought and blurted, "What do you plan to discuss with my husband? You are making it sound quite entangled."

"Nothing to cause you any further problems," he said. "In fact it might be better if I see you both together."

Helen made no attempt to conceal her sigh of relief. It was agreed that she and Steve would come together for the next hour.

Dr. Odell opened the door to the waiting room at exactly five o'clock and did not hide his blink of surprise to find Helen and her husband settled into chairs thumbing through magazines. He made a great thing of looking at his watch and drawled, "Surprise! Right on time. Your husband must have a good influence on you." He turned and offered his hand to Steve. "Mr. James, I'm Dr. Odell. Won't you come in?"

They arose and Dr. Odell noted that Steve was at least six feet two inches tall with a build that was a bit too lanky to be called athletic. He had the firm handshake and the ready smile of a salesman. He was well dressed, well groomed, and looked successful and confident. Somehow he was not as Dr. Odell had pictured him.

The doctor followed them into the office and closed the door behind them. Helen quickly dived possessively into her accustomed chair next to the doctor, leaving Steve standing looking rather hesitant.

"Please sit in the chair by your wife," the doctor said, indicating. "It'll make it easier for all to talk to each other." He made a mental note that Helen's attitude toward her husband was that of competitiveness for the therapist's attention.

"It seems so strange to have a third person in here," Helen said nervously.

"I didn't intend to make you uncomfortable, dear," Steve said, looking solicitously at his wife. "I had hoped for the opposite."

"I didn't mean that you are making me uncomfortable exactly, Steve. It just seems peculiar—I'm so

accustomed to being here alone with Dr. Odell."
(Damn him. We haven't been here two minutes and
I'm already defending myself. How dare he look so
concerned about my welfare. It's an act to sway Dr.
Odell over to his side and make me seem complaining
and bitchy.)

Dr. Odell thought about whether or not to comment on their little interaction and decided against it.
"I'm glad you came today, Mr. James."

"Call me Steve. Everybody does."

(That's right, Doctor, just call him good-old-
buddy Steve. Everybody likes good old Steve. Everybody is on a first-name basis with him. He is just one
of the guys. Everybody gets along with him—but me.)

"All right, Steve," the doctor said. He did not
really feel on a first-name basis yet, but he decided to
comply with Steve's wish. "I asked Helen to invite
you in because I believe it might be a help to Helen
directly or indirectly. Perhaps you can tell me some
things about Helen that I don't know, and also you
might understand a little more of what goes on in
here with your wife and how she reacts."

"I certainly am willing to do anything I can to
help her get over this current upset, Doctor. In fact,
I canceled an important meeting this afternoon to
come along with her." He glanced at his watch. "The
meeting should be over just about now."

"You never mentioned any meeting to me,"
Helen said. (I'll bet it's only their routine Tuesday
afternoon sales meeting which he skips half the time
and groans about attending the other half.)

"I didn't want to worry you about it, honey," Steve said smoothly. "After all, this is certainly more important isn't it?" His tone indicated he thought it was not.

As this exchange was occurring, Dr. Odell began to be dubious. Steve seemed a little too glib and over-solicitous. He quickly reviewed in his own mind the main points that he wished to cover with Helen's husband. He wished to get a quick estimate of Steve's strengths and weaknesses; he wanted Steve's version of their marital problems and what Steve considered to be Helen's problems; he needed actual knowledge of what Steve was like so that if Helen got carried away in her vivid descriptions of her husband, he could keep his perspective; and finally he wanted to pave the way for Steve to have further contact with him if it were necessary. Once you have met someone, it's much easier to call him if you are upset or worried. He decided to start with the least threatening line of questions.

"From your point of view, Steve, what seems to have been troubling Helen lately?" Dr. Odell asked.

Steve glanced at Helen as if to ask permission to speak.

"Well, go ahead," Helen said. "Now's your chance." (I want to be here when you, a grown and supposedly responsible adult male, tell the good doctor about how your wife has not had the foresight to make the family investments. I wish to hear with my own ears as you admit to a third party that you'd like to financially strap us so you can fly about the countryside in a private airplane. And don't forget to tell him what a waste of our money my therapy is.)

Steve was still hesitant. "I think perhaps Helen just takes things a little too seriously. Some small incident happens and she blows it up out of all proportion until she actually makes herself sick. She cries over nothing at all. But I have no real complaints. I know she'll pull out of this." He smiled encouragingly at his wife.

"Are you saying you think that Helen is overly sensitive and overly emotional?" the doctor asked.

"Why are you both talking about me in the third person?" Helen asked. "You act as if I'm not here."

"I haven't forgotten you," Dr. Odell said. "From the way your husband looks at you before he speaks, I don't think he has forgotten either."

"What was your question again, Doctor?" Steve asked, ignoring Helen's outburst.

"Besides Helen being overly emotional, what is your version of why she is coming to see me and is willing at this point to spend a substantial amount of time and money?"

Steve was silent. He once again glanced at Helen, but it was obvious that he was reticent to speak frankly in front of her. "Helen is sort of a generally uptight person, Dr. Odell. She always has been and probably always will be. If she doesn't have something to worry about, she invents something. Her mother is the same way, and probably her mother's mother. Helen is a third generation worrier."

"That's right, it's just a congenital defect, isn't it, dear?" Helen said acidly. "Something over which I have no control—sort of like a club foot or crossed eyes. So certainly I shouldn't be spending any money to overcome it!" Tears of anger welled in her eyes.

"See what I mean, Doctor," said Steve, turning to his wife. "Helen, I knew it would be like this if I came. Everything I say these days is wrong. I was sure nothing good would come of my being here today, and I was right. You must understand I'm not saying these things to upset you. I'm only trying to help you by telling Dr. Odell the truth." He glanced at his watch again, and for the first time seemed ill at ease himself.

"The truth as you see it, Steven James! You're trying to drag my whole family into it, two generations back yet." She reached for a Kleenex and furiously dabbed at her eyes.

Dr. Odell made several further abortive attempts to get some useful and specific information, but with Steve's vague responses and Helen's constant interruptions, he was making little progress. He began to form an idea of the nature of their fruitless arguments. Although it seemed a little risky with Helen already feeling excluded, he decided to gamble on seeing Steve alone for the remainder of the session. He asked Helen to step into the waiting room with him.

"Helen, would you permit me to talk to him a short time alone? He's anything but enthusiastic about being here, and this might be my only chance to know him better. If he could accept me even a little, he might be more receptive toward your therapy and might show me some hidden strengths which could help you later."

"All right, fine," Helen said glumly. "I was getting a little bored at being treated as if I weren't there anyway. I'll just go around the corner and have a fattening ice cream soda. Please tell Steve to pick me up there when you two are through talking about me," she smiled weakly.

"Okay. I'll see you next week—and don't use your imagination too much between now and then."

"Who? Me? Doctor, you know I don't even have one," she said as she left.

The doctor went back into his office and explained to Steve. "I thought it might be easier for you to talk if Helen weren't here. She will be waiting for you at the corner drug store. I did notice you kept looking at her as if you didn't want to hurt her feelings or were afraid she would be offended."

"Hell, she was offended. No matter what I do or say these days she's offended. I don't understand what's gotten into her, Doctor." He pulled his chair a bit closer to the doctor's in a man-to-man attitude. "You know how it is, Doc. All women—my mother, my sister, my wife—they all have these periods of unreasonableness. I sometimes wonder if it has something to do with their glands."

Dr. Odell gave up in his attempt to elicit more spontaneous information. He decided to inquire about a known specific problem. "Wasn't there some kind of an argument about an airplane around the time this all started?" he asked.

"Oh, that," Steve said. "Yes, I'd almost forgotten. That's a perfect illustration of what I'm talking about. I have just catered to her whims too much. The particular night of that argument I came home and found a bill from Goldwater's for $100 worth of shoes. That same day I had been offered a chance to get in on a deal to buy half interest in a plane.

"I'm in the air conditioning business, you know, and it would certainly give me a jump on my competitors if I could fly parts to the outlying desert areas. The extra commissions would probably pay for the plane over a period of time. The family could have used it on weekends, too. When I mentioned it to Helen she burst out in a rage and absolutely refused to discuss it. After accusing me of having extravagant ideas, she went out the next day and bought a big fancy Lincoln. Now that's feminine logic for you!" He sat back waiting.

Dr. Odell scratched his head and wondered what tack to take next. Although Steve's words appeared logical, Dr. Odell was forming a negative opinion of him. He could imagine himself writing a personality description which stated that Steve was "superficial, uninvolved, self-centered, unperceptive, and manipulating." He mentally contrasted him with the husband of another patient he had seen recently who was obviously worried and concerned about his

wife, could describe many specific changes in the last
six months, and had volunteered to go into a marital
group.

"How did she feel after she bought the car?" the
doctor asked. His intention now was not to make a
judgment as to whose story was correct but to find
out about Steve's perception of his wife's feelings at
the beginning of her current emotional upset.

"Well, she seemed upset. She was certainly no
more upset about it than I was. How would you feel,
Doc, if you came home one night and discovered that
your wife had gone out and bought a fancy Lincoln
that day without discussing it with you?"

"Didn't you have to sign some papers with her?"
the doctor asked. He was curious to learn if Steve
would take the responsibility for his own behavior or
blame Helen again.

"Hell, yes, I signed them. I didn't have much
choice. The car was already parked in the garage and
she had arranged the loan with the bank. Everything
was done up in a neat little bundle waiting for me to
sign on the dotted line. What else could I do? Refuse
and listen to her bitch endlessly about my new car
and her old one? No thanks." His eyes did not meet
the doctor's during this exchange. In contrast to his
complaining words, his expression was self-satisfied.
"You know, when she spent the money on the car, it
ended any hope I had of investing in the plane."

"How disappointing was that you you?" Dr.
Odell asked.

"It was very disappointing at first. I've gotten

over it now, however. You have to learn to get over disappointments if you are married to Helen." His voice still did not convey the slightest bitterness but seemed remarkably casual.

"Have you been pretty disillusioned with Helen during your marriage? How unhappy are you?"

"I wouldn't say 'disillusioned' and 'unhappy' are exactly the words I would choose. They're a little too strong." He smiled disarmingly. "I suppose I'd just say that marriage hasn't been exactly what I expected. I imagine that's true for most everybody."

"What are your worst disappointments?" the doctor asked gently.

"Well, I'll tell you. I feel that I'm a pretty damned good husband. I make a hell of a lot more money than the average man and just hand over my paycheck to her. I've done more remodeling and repairs to our house than any six men I know. I don't screw around with other women, I don't gamble, and I don't beat her. I tolerate a lot of foolish conversation from her without saying a word. You know, Helen's never had it so good. I even let her make the rules for the kids without interfering. She gets to handle all the money. It's been so long since I wrote one of our checks I'm not sure I'd even remember how. She makes most of our social arrangements, and I'll go along with about anything she wants. Does all this make her happy? No. She constantly badgers me to 'talk to her' or to plan a surprise evening out.' No matter what I give it's not enough. All I want from her is what every man wants—a little true consideration from a wife."

"What could Helen do that would make you feel this true consideration?"

Steve paused. "Hell, not much really. My tastes are very simple. I admit to being a little particular about the house being clean all the time. Is it too much to expect a decent dinner to be on the table when I get home at night? And to have a little peace and quiet before I go to bed? Or to have clean shirts and underwear? You know, since Helen has been in this spell of hers, one morning I didn't even have a clean pair of shorts to wear to work. I just don't think I'm asking a hell of a lot from her."

Dr. Odell noticed that Steve did not mention the fact that Helen also had a full-time job. However, he felt that if Steve had to be reminded, it was a waste of time to point it out. Steve was beginning to remind him of one of his teen-age patients, a boy of sixteen. As this thought crossed his mind, he decided to enter the conversation at a new level and follow it through. Temporarily thinking of Steve as a sixteen-year-old, he asked, "Does she let you have a night out with the boys without a long explanation?"

"If I want a night out, I just don't come home. Sometimes I call her and tell her I'm working late. I know she'd give me the third degree if I told her I was going out for a few drinks with some of the guys. You know, there are times when I just need some conversation with other men, and this is the only time I get it. Then when I get home Helen wants to know where I've been, what I've been doing, and why they are so much more interesting to talk to than she is. I must admit—sometimes an evening out isn't worth it."

Dr. Odell was beginning to realize that Steve saw Helen not as a wife or even as a friend, certainly not as a confidante to whom he could tell his private thoughts and feelings as he apparently did to his more casual buddies. In Steve's mind his wife seemed to be a strong maternal figure who was necessary for his comfort and security but at the same time was too restrictive and demanding of him.

"I notice you haven't said anything about your sex life," the doctor said.

Steve looked slightly uncomfortable and grinned sheepishly. "She takes pretty good care of me usually," he said, not meeting the doctor's gaze. "She sure hasn't been much in bed lately though—ever since this emotional trouble of hers started. She just doesn't seem to be interested."

"One more thing, Mr. James—Steve. When you decided to marry Helen, what was there about her that made you choose her? Maybe you could describe Helen as you remember her before you were married."

"That's been a long time ago. It's hard to remember," Steve answered. "Of course, she was pretty good-looking—pretty well stacked, too. She had a good sense of humor and even seemed kind of silly and giggly sometimes but I knew that she was a smart girl with a good head on her shoulders. She played the piano a lot in those days, you know. She joked about it, but there was no doubt she was serious about her

music. Sometimes I had to wait for her to finish practicing when I came to pick her up for a date. She was
a responsible girl. She always had a job after school
and on Saturdays and she was a fanatic about paying
her bills on time."

His voice had softened and his expression had
become pensive as he remembered his courtship days
with Helen. "You know, Doc, I do love her, but I
don't know what the hell's happened to her. I'm the
same as always but she seems to be going downhill."

After this recital Dr. Odell wondered what in
the world Helen had seen in Steve. He determined
that he would put the same question to Helen at their
next appointment.

"I see our time is about up," the doctor said. "I
do want to throw out a couple more thoughts to you.
I want to consider the possibility that later you might
want to see a therapist yourself or join a marital
group. Your wife may get so angry or so confusing
to you that you might feel the need for help. Many
husbands do under these circumstances. It is quite
normal for Helen to show some healthy changes that
might upset you."

Dr. Odell knew as he watched Steve's facial expression that his words were a lost cause. Still he
said, "If this should happen, or you get concerned
about Helen, please call me."

"Yes, I'll do that, but I doubt if it will come up,"
Steve answered, dismissing any possibility of such an
event. "Helen's a good soldier and all I want is for her

to be the way she was before this Fall. I don't think she'll have much trouble getting back on her feet."

The doctor walked with Steve to the door. Steve's attitude was that of one who has done his duty and wants to forget it quickly. His last words were, "If the kids weren't already home from school, I'd take her out to dinner tonight. She doesn't like to cook, you know. Maybe we'll do it later in the week."

After he had gone, Dr. Odell sat in his chair and shook his head. In his notes Dr. Odell wrote for the hour:

Steven James at first appearance looks success-ful, confident, and is a rather handsome, quite virile-appearing man. He is the type of husband with whom many wives think they could find complete happi-ness and yet somehow end up unexplainably frus-trated. Mr. James is intelligent, has above average earnings, is not sickly, does not chase other women, does not gamble or drink to excess, does not physi-cally abuse his wife. He is a good handyman around the house. He is sexually adequate and, in addition to the above attributes, he professes to love his wife. Yet Helen obviously feels very unloved, untrusting, overburdened, and insecure. Unfortunately, this interview strongly supports a very real basis for Helen's feelings. The truth is that Mr. James is, despite his surface appearance, an infantile man whose psychological development resembles that of an adolescent male. He wants and has arranged for his wife to be almost totally responsible for the major decisions in the family, which allows him to remain more of a child rather than an adult male. While he professes to be doing his wife-mother a favor, he actually had delegated to her all financial matters, the rules and discipline for the children and arrangement of their social life, in addition to expecting a very well-run household.

He completely ignores the fact of her full-time job in terms of his expectations of her. He sees his responsibilities fulfilled by turning his paycheck over to her and by doing handy work around the house. Helen is not yet able even to describe her need for intimacy and the sharing of private feelings with her husband, a real need which is not being met at all.

It is exceedingly apparent that Steve is unable as well as unwilling to trust Helen with any important inner feelings or emotional intimacy, even denying the existence of any secret emotions about shame, weakness, hostility, or fear and discouraging Helen's discussing her own such feelings. He can only woodenly play the role of the "good boy" or the "manly man." In a childlike fashion he wants all the care and protection offered by a strong but kindly mother, yet completely rejects this same mother who places any unwanted restrictions or demands on him.

Helen was destined by her childhood to have emotional problems, and her relationship with her husband has served to exaggerate them. At the present time Mr. James shows absolutely no potential and no motivation for marital group therapy or for individual psychotherapy. He likes things just the way they *were in the recent past. The only way he would be likely to get treatment would be if Helen became healthy enough that he were unable to continue to blame and manipulate her. It is doubtful that Helen realizes how able her opponent is, her husband being an expert, if unaware, guilt manipulator, capitalizing on her guilt feelings to subtly force her to give him what he wants.*

CHAPTER 10

Dr. Odell was not surprised when Helen was ten minutes late for her next appointment following Steve's visit to the office. What he was not prepared for, however, was the change in her. For the first time since he had known her, she manifested the depressed state that she had often described to him. The change in her did not take the more classic form of neglectfulness in her appearance and grooming; rather the reverse was true. It was as if she had used her last bit of energy and strength to carefully groom herself in an effort to convince the world of her invulnerability. Her efforts failed dismally for the effect was that of a high-styled mannikin on display in a shop window.

He walked to the waiting room and greeted her, and when she raised her eyes they did not meet his but stopped at the level of his tie. She rose and followed him wordlessly into his office. Instead of falling casually into her usual chair while giving numerous excuses for being late, she sat down sedately and appeared to wait with a vague, preoccupied smile.

Dr. Odell automatically pushed the ash tray toward her, because she ordinarily spent her first few moments of the session digging through the paraphernalia in her huge handbag for cigarettes and matches, chattering all the while. Today, however, she calmly opened her bag, found her cigarettes and matches immediately, and carefully closed her purse. She lit a cigarette, inhaled deeply, and said nothing.

Dr. Odell thought of several subtle openings but discarded these to bluntly say, "What the hell's the matter with you?"

"I don't know what you mean," she said, still not meeting his gaze.

"Come on, don't stall around with me. You can't even look me in the eye."

She immediately met his gaze directly and coldly, but did not speak.

"So now you can look at me, but you've still lost your voice and apparently all your feelings, too."

"Oh, no, I haven't lost my feelings," she said, and her voice broke immediately. "I just don't think I can possibly talk about them to you." (Especially not to you! You traitor! Saboteur! Untrustworthy side with husbands. Not that I really blame you—I just feel like taking the Fifth Amendment today. Miserable as I am, I don't yet feel like aiding in my own downfall.)

"This is a big change since I last saw you. What's happened anyway?" Dr. Odell wondered what Steve might have told her about their session together which led to her depression and obvious mistrust.

He started to feel guilty and chagrined, wondering if it had been a total mistake to include her husband before she had developed real trust in her therapist.

"Nothing actually has happened," she answered, and now tears began to flow freely. "It isn't worth discussing anyway. These days I seem to take very minor events much too seriously and get them all out of proportion." Her voice rose and became an uncontrolled wail at the end of her sentence and she blew her nose soundly.

"Did you talk over what happened last hour with Steve?"

Helen sobbed and seemed unable to gain control of herself. Her reaction in itself was an answer, and Dr. Odell felt a surge of sympathy for her. He slid his chair closer to her and said softly, "I know you are hurting badly today. Don't forget that I'm a friend and I'm right here now."

Helen flinched away from him. "Please don't do that. Please don't say that kind of thing when you don't mean it." Her voice was pleading. "You must know it only makes it worse." (Don't you know that you are the cause of my falling apart? Are you really so blind as to think I would believe you are my friend? Steve's maybe; not mine.)

"Baloney! I see you are still trying to tell me how I feel. Stop trying to believe that I don't care about you."

She faced him fully now, steadfastly meeting his eyes and said, "I wish I could. I truly wish I could. I don't know who or what to believe anymore."

"I can tell you one thing to believe," he answered. "I do care about you and I know that you are in pain."

"You'll have to understand that this entire situation is very difficult for me." Her voice had gained some control and she went on. "I want to confide in you, but I am so scared. It is as if I am paying for you to be my friend for an hour at a time, and I keep thinking of how I will feel when I leave here. I will go on feeling desperate and you'll go on to worrying about helping your next patient, forgetting all about me until next time at five o'clock. That just isn't enough for me. I'm sorry." (I need you but you don't need me. It makes the relationship unequal and untrustworthy.)

"That's just another way of saying you don't think I care enough. I say it again. I do care. Now tell me how miserable you really do feel."

"I feel so damned lousy I'm not sure I'm worth your trouble to find out why. I just feel so *worthless!* My mind goes round and round and I end up wondering why, if I really am so worthless, I should put so much effort into trying to find out why. Does that make any sense to you?" Her voice was tired, as if it took a great effort on her part to try to put her thoughts into words.

"The sense it makes to me is that you have over reacted to the whole damned scene with Steve and you and me. I suppose it was a big mistake on my part even to have him come in."

"Oh, I don't think learning the truth about oneself is ever a mistake. There are some facets of my personality I might never have discovered had it not been through Steve and his little chat with you," she answered acidly. (Like how you sat together and agreed that I am an overemotional slob, amplifying every event in my life to put myself in the martyr role.) Her voice cracked again as she continued, "I can still see the two of you together, good-naturedly enjoying a man-to-man talk about what a poor, weak, sick creature I am." (Damn you both! I came here to get help for my trouble with one man—not to get more of it from another.)

"Helen, I hope you know you're annoying the hell out of me. You seem to be trying to prove that you are the very kind of creature that your husband prefers to think that you are, an overly emotional, nervous, senseless woman who has mysterious changes in mood for no good reason at all. What I really think is . . ."

"I don't give a damn what you really think. You sound exactly like Steve now. That last little speech could have been from his own mouth. It's the game he plays—one called 'See What I Mean.' When I feel totally down the tube, worthless, hopeless, and unable to explain why, I naively think it will help if I can talk to him. Sometimes in the middle of my struggle of trying to describe to him the waves of despair that are engulfing me, he becomes so bored he picks up the newspaper. This gesture becomes the final proof my my worthlessness and I admit that I do get emotional.

"I mean I'm practically pouring out my life's

blood to him hoping he can somehow help me pull out of the tunnel I'm in. At this point he turns back from his newspaper and informs me that he can't possibly talk sensibly with me when I am so emotionally overwrought. This has the predictable effect on me, because I'm sure that I do go quite insane at this remark which literally drives me up a tree. Then he sits back smugly while I cry and storm and says, 'See what I mean.' It's a nasty little game I don't intend to play with you, too."

"Then why don't you stop it. Before you interrupted me I was about to say that it's very obvious to me that you are far more a real human being than your husband is. If you would stop to think for even a moment you could remember how much and how often I talk about 'feelings.' In fact I believe you have good reason to feel very exasperated and depressed by your husband's behavior."

"You have just made the entire situation seem utterly hopeless. As long as I thought my feelings about Steve were in my head, there seemed a chance to straighten out my thinking. Now you tell me the feelings are real—there seems no place to go from here."

"You have the knack of making me feel like a son-of-a-bitch no matter what I say to you today. It may make you feel temporarily hopeless to realize the truth about your marriage but it puts you in a better position to actually deal with your life—what the hell did he tell you anyway about our talk together while you were gone?"

"He said the two of you got on quite well together — 'saw eye-to-eye' I believe is the way he put it. He seemed to feel that you were in perfect agreement that I am overemotional, bossy, pushy, and controlling, and demanding. He described how sympathetic you looked when he told you about his disappointment over the airplane." She paused and swallowed hard. "He also said you told him he should contact you right away when I fall apart." Now she reached for the Kleenex and wept openly.

"Helen, I do have much mixed feelings about you now. I feel sympathetic in the same way I would toward any good friend who is in misery, but I also feel exasperated because you are so persistent in not trusting me and believing that I have taken sides against you. To be perfectly truthful with you, I really did not even feel inclined to sympathize with Steve, let alone openly agree and commiserate with him. As far as telling him to call me when you fall apart, this is not what I said at all. My exact words were that you might make some changes that would be healthy for you but upsetting to him. I suggested that it might be helpful to him to see a therapist himself or join a marital group. Did he mention these suggestions to you?"

Helen smiled for the first time since she had arrived. "I think I got an edited version," she said. (I wonder if some of Steve's other recitations to me aren't "edited" in the same manner. There's a ring of familiarity. I wonder if he does it intentionally.)

"I think you got depressed when you felt you could no longer trust me and believed I had betrayed you by agreeing with your husband." Dr. Odell felt he might be premature in correlating her depression with a loss of trust in him, but it seemed worth a gamble. If Helen could see her desperate need to trust and confide in someone and he could convince her that he was trustworthy, the toughest part of therapy would be over.

"I didn't get depressed. I got *more* depressed."

"If you are depressed when you don't trust me, why not take a chance on really telling me how you feel?"

"Because I am afraid I will begin to need you more and more and become totally dependent on you. I just can't stand the idea of myself as a spineless, clinging child hanging onto her therapist's apron strings. You see, until you need someone or feel close to them, they do not have the capability of hurting you. It's because you don't *care*. I am afraid to *care* about you—or your opinion of me. Does that in any way make it clear to you why I am afraid to let you any closer? Because at any moment you wish you can say, 'I'm sorry but I am unable to see you anymore. See someone else. I have filled this time.' Or, 'You are really not a very good patient at all and you don't try to work very hard on your problems, so unless you can change you ways, please don't come back.' I feel that trusting or depending on someone in the way you invite me to is the same as putting my head on the block and handing you the ax."

"Obviously your head would be perfectly safe. I have no desire to harm you."

"It's not the *desire* to harm me that is my concern—it's the *capacity* to harm me."

"Does that mean that by trusting me you will be giving me the capacity to hurt you or disappoint you?" he asked.

"Exactly. I couldn't have said it better myself," she answered, not meeting his eyes.

"Yet you are hurting yourself all the time by being lonely and untrusting. Of course, you may feel more in control by your self-inflicted pain." He felt so annoyed with her continued rejection that he had to stifle the impulse to shake her.

"Control! There's that word again. I believe that is one of the words you used when you and Steve discussed me. In fact that little speech you just made sounded rehearsed. I wonder if you just said it to your last patient, too. How dull and boring psychotherapy must be for you—to have to repeat over and over the same dull lines every hour."

"Bullshit! Quit reading my mind so incorrectly. I know how I feel. I am not bored. I am angry. Now do us both a favor and concentrate on how *you* feel, not how you think I feel."

"I'm sorry. I really do apologize for accusing you of playacting. I just feel so terrible and jumpy and tired and mean. So totally hopeless." Her expression was one of total exhaustion now, or giving up. "I think I could stand it if I knew when it would end. I could gird myself for a week or a month, but it just seems a hopeless cause. If it has gone on this long, perhaps it could go on for years. Even if I ever do get 'well'—whatever that is—then I'll have to look back over all the time I wasted in miserable nothingness. If I could only put my finger on what exactly is bothering me, I could begin to cope with it. I feel like a cipher, a nothing, but if I were really such a cipher, why would I carry on so about it?"

The depth of her depression jarred him into abrupt awareness that she simply had to be having suicidal thoughts. It suddenly worried him that she had not mentioned them. The person who secretly clutches self-destructive thoughts to himself is far more in danger than the one who can admit them openly to the therapist.

"It comes to mind as you say that, you never have told me anything about suicidal thoughts or feelings," he said. "As far as I can tell, I have more thoughts like that than you do."

"I can't believe this is me sitting here discussing suicide," she said almost in a whisper. (Good old strong Helen. Never let anything get her down. "Go on and try, honey, you can do anything you set your mind to." Isn't that what Mother always told me. And Steve, too. "You're always so resourceful, Helen; nothing seems to defeat you." And myself. I've even done that to myself. If the problem seemed too big to cope with, I denied that it existed. Until recently I could have had a herd of wild elephants charging me and simply stood in their path and shouted, "I do not believe in you, elephants," and *known* that they would either vanish or turn and retreat. Not now. Now I am too tired. Now I *am* defeated.)

Dr. Odell interrupted her reverie. "Suicide does seem unreal but most intelligent people do think about it at one time or another. I know I have. In my suicidal thoughts, however, I usually plan on taking someone with me." He realized it was quite frightening to her to think about suicide. By admitting his own self-destructive thoughts, he hoped that perhaps he could lift the taboo she felt about openly discussing her own.

"Yours must be a more advanced form," she said and managed a shadow of a smile. "My own seem to be concerned with me alone." Her eyes had become more swollen and red rimmed as the hour progressed, and she appeared bereft as she faced him squarely and continued: "Life has become to me a silly, useless waste of time. I wonder who ever invented life anyway? A great practical joker. And what does any of it mean except something to get through somehow. I can't seem to dredge up enough energy even to think seriously of doing myself in. I think more of myself as harmless but crawling along the floor who isn't even worth stepping on."

"Concretely, in what way have you thought about doing yourself in?" he asked her gently. He was aware that while she was bringing up true depressive feelings, she was avoiding any mention of a practical plan. He wanted to make her talk about it as thoroughly as he could, for the more she actually confided in him any details of her plan, the less likely she was to try to put them into effect.

"Let me think about it a minute." (I mustn't tell him about the motel plan. That ultimate cop-out is for my own private, secret self alone. That is my money in the bank.) "Actually," she said, "it isn't so much of a concrete plan as it is many such rambling ideas. I don't sleep well—you'd never have guessed, would you?—and I sort of slink around the house during the wee hours and contemplate first one way and then another." (Like the peace that must exist at the bottom of a swimming pool or the final state produced by many pink and yellow and red capsules—or the contemplation of one's own brains smeared on the living room ceiling.)

"Tell me one of them."

"God, this is a depressing subject," she said. "Can't we talk about something else for a while. I know you probably think you're making me feel better by talking about it, but such is not the case, I can assure you." She looked at her watch. "Also my hour is over."

"I'm not that inflexible, he said. "I do have that feeling of incompleteness . . . "

"I know the feeling. I've had it many times as I left here. However, I did abide by your rules and left when you told me the hour was up. I think we should stick by your rules now, too." (I must be sicker than I thought if he's willing to break his own fifty-minute rule.)

"Now you're acting bitchy again, so it's hard to believe you're that depressed."

"Believe it or don't; it's your choice," she said as she gathered her cigarettes and matches and put them in her purse.

"It just so happens that I like to get phone calls from bitchy women," he said as they both rose from their chairs. "I do worry about you, so please call me if things don't get any better."

To his vast relief, she relaxed and smiled. "May I?" she asked. "I've often wanted to, you know, but I didn't think it was the thing to do—against the rules again, I suppose. It seemed unfair to ask you for time when I wasn't paying you."

"If you feel really desperate, please call me. God knows, I'm all too aware that you are not likely to abuse the privilege. Don't forget, my number is . . . "

"Oh, I know your number," she said. "Sometimes when I can't sleep and I'm at my worst, like at two or three o'clock in the morning, it has helped me just to look you up in the phone book."

"Good. I'm glad you think about me when you really need a friend." He had a kind thought for the telephone company.

"Oh, I do," she said and then shyly added. "I've even written you letters. Of course, I throw them away. Pouring out my rancid soul on paper to you has in fact been my salvation on several occasions. The writing of them—not your reading them—has been quite therapeutic."

He remembered her written autobiography and how well she had expressed her emotions on paper.

"Don't throw anything more away that you write until we talk about it."

"I can't promise that," she said. "Maybe I don't even write them to you; maybe I write them to God." At last she grinned, and it was a facsimile of her old familiar smile. "You wouldn't want to read somebody else's mail now, would you?"

The momentary return to her bantering ways did not entirely distract him from this sudden and newfound knowledge that she had been carrying on an interaction with him unbeknown to him. She knew his telephone number. She had written him letters — apparently letters whose contents she was still hiding from him. He didn't like it. She undoubtedly endowed the Dr. Odell of her letters with qualities that would ultimately lead to her own misery. It was too late to discuss it with her today, but he intended to take it up again.

"It sounds more to me as if I'm not even getting to read my own mail. Send it to me next time—or bring it with you."

"We'll see—maybe for Christmas."

"And call me if you need to."

"I will."

The hour with Dr. Odell lifted the weight of gloom from Helen for one night. Even that night she was aware that her depression was barely held at bay. Her session with the doctor had partially anesthetized her; she knew the pain was still there but she could not feel it so sharply. It allowed her to get a much needed full night's sleep.

It was the next day when the torturing, foreboding feelings returned in full force. She mechanically led herself to the office and struggled through the first half of the day. The Christmas decorations and constant holiday references served to convince her that all the world was joyous except herself.

When she could stand her own thoughts no longer and she was sure Tom would be away from his desk for at least an hour to keep an appointment with his accountant, thus insuring her privacy, she gingerly picked up the phone. It shook in her hand. With trembling fingers, she dialed Dr. Odell's number.

One ring. She waited, holding her breath. She really shouldn't call him but simply ought to wait two more days until her next appointment. Two rings. Two more days. She was sure the pounding of her heart and the heavy gloom that was settling over her would destroy her long before then. Three rings. (He isn't there! Well, what did you expect, you dimwit? Haven't you learned by now that no one is ever there when you . . .)

"Dr. Odell's office," said the feminine voice into the receiver. The shock of hearing an answer when she had prepared herself for rejection was so startling she actually jumped.

"Is Dr. Odell in, please?" she asked, forcing calmness into her voice.

"I'm sorry. He's with a patient right now. May I have him call you?"

Helen left her name and number and sighed with relief as she hung up the phone. Now she would have time to organize her thoughts before he returned the call. Besides somehow now when he called her back, it would be more as if he were contacting her rather than vice versa. She looked at her watch. One thirty. He wouldn't be calling before one fifty when his break came before his two o'clock appointment. She was able to calm the pounding of her heart and still the shaking of her hands enough to begin typing Tom's dictation.

As one fifty approached she began to eye the phone. The trembling in her hands returned and they became clammy. What will I tell him when he does call? (My God, what have I done? I'll just start crying —right here in the office—and I won't be able to tell him what is wrong because I don't even know myself. Maybe the secretary won't give him the message.) She discounted the idea, however, because Helen had far more faith in secretaries than in most other people and trusted that Dr. Odell would get the message.

Two o'clock. (Maybe he is running late with his patient.) Five minutes past two. (He probably won't call me until his next break.)

By three o'clock when the doctor still had not returned her call, she was unable to accomplish any task more demanding than filing. She shuffled papers on her desk, then reshuffled them back the way they were. Tears were trying to squeeze through her eyes.

At three thirty when Tom returned to the office from his appointment, he took one look at her and said, "Helen, what in the world is wrong? You look ghastly. Are you sick?"

"Not really, Tom. A slight headache, that's all." How inane, she thought. A slight headache—what a stupid excuse. (What should I tell him? I am a madwoman having some sort of fatal attack which may leave me a lobotomized vegetable but my own doctor can't spare the time to return a telephone call? I have a sudden case of brain tumor which has destroyed my IQ and palsied my limbs? I have just steeled myself to call someone to ask for help, which is the biggest mistake in my life thus far because my so-called saviour is too busy to be bothered by anyone?)

"I really think you should go home, Helen. You look as if you're coming down with something," Tom said with concern. "Besides if you are, I don't want to catch it," he added, smiling good-humoredly. "Go on home now, and don't come in tomorrow unless you feel better. Want me to drive you?"

"No thanks, Tom. But thank you. I think if you can get along without me, I will go home. I seem to feel quite out of it."

But she did not go home. She wasn't sure if her legs would hold her up all the way down the elevator and to the garage where her car was parked. She beat it to the ladies room down the hall barely managing to hold the tears back until the door closed behind her.

Why, why, why did I ever call him in the first place, she cried. The tears accelerated and became sobs. What could he possibly have done even if he had called back? (I should know by now that you are only asking for trouble when you depend on someone else. Oh, boy, how he set you up, Helen, you stupid, stupid woman. "Depend on me, Helen." Damn his black soul to hell! Sure, old buddy, I can depend on you from five to six o'clock on Mondays and Thursdays. Isn't that the way the game goes? But just forget about such nonsense on a Tuesday afternoon at one thirty. That is the time for someone else to rely and depend on him.) She had broken the rules. He undoubtedly had a list fourteen pages long of patients who were waiting to see him who would keep his lousy, stupid, goddamned, son-of-a-bitching therapy rules! Well, he could most assuredly put the top name on his list in her appointment time. She hoped he would rot in hell for all eternity and she would never have to lay eyes on him again. Double talk—he was full of shitty, lying double talk.

She suddenly realized she felt considerably better. She didn't need him. She had certainly survived and prospered before she ever laid eyes on him. (Him and that bearded, game-playing "Tell me how you feel now" Steinberg. They were a pair! A matched set. A plague on both their houses!)

She felt revitalized as her anger pumped energy back into her veins. If Tom could have seen her as she strode from the ladies room on her way to the elevator, he would have been hard pressed to recognize her as the "sick" secretary he had sent home twenty minutes earlier.

Her anger sustained her all evening. She hadn't felt this good since before Steve had gone for his appointment with Dr. Odell. She was sufficiently aware of her own reaction to wish she could remain angry all the time to ward off the nightmarish terror and descending blackness that came over her at other times. If she could just stay mad as hell, she would be all right.

Her reprieve again was to last only overnight. By morning the invisible, suffocating, hurtling-towards-doom sensations had returned, and her feelings had reversed themselves. She puzzled over what metamorphoses took place with her as she slept. It was the same sort of emotional turnabout which always engulfed her after an argument with Steve. She no longer felt anger at Dr. Odell, only sympathy.

(Who can blame him? I certainly wouldn't return a call to me if I could think of a way to get out of it.) With a thud she wondered if that was his way of telling her he didn't want to see her anymore. She couldn't blame him for that either. (What a dull, uninteresting, gloomy blob I am. *But who the hell can tell me how I can get away from myself!*)

CHAPTER 11

Helen's depression continued throughout the holiday season. She never mentioned to Dr. Odell that she had tried to call him or sought an explanation for his "neglectful" behavior. In fact, she clutched his rejection to herself as proof of his untrustworthiness. During her sessions with him she managed to show just enough humor and self-assertion that he did not seriously consider having her hospitalized. Each time before her arrival he found himself rehearsing a speech referring her to a hospital psychiatrist in case the need might arise. For these weeks, from December into February, they each walked their separate tightropes. Nothing he could do altered their relationship in a more solid direction.

Dr. Odell reviewed the established methods of treating depressed patients and worked them into their hours together. He reminded her of past accomplishments for Helen seemed convinced that she had never achieved success in any endeavor. He cited examples of her success in music, in her career, and

with her children. She countered with an almost convincing series of arguments to the effect that any idiot
could have done what she had done given the same
circumstances.

His second method was to remind her of previous depressive episodes and of the fact that they
always had a beginning and an end. He was trying to
reassure her that she would feel better in the future,
that she would return to a happier state of mind as she
had in the past. He asked her to try to remember such
depressive periods in her past. She recalled her feelings of loss when her pet dog died and when she left
home for college. She was not able to tie these episodes
into her present feelings at all, stating that it was different now; she knew what was wrong those other
times and now she hadn't the faintest idea.

How could you fight an invisible enemy? The
doctor pointed out that he could help make her enemy
more visible, but she passively remained unconvinced.
He desperately tried to provoke her into anger, knowing that ultimately her depression would have to be
translated into anger and vented. His attempts were
futile. Helen either smiled wryly at his provocations
or agreed with his manufactured criticisms.

He made efforts to "model" for Helen, to
demonstrate to her how to become angry for no good
reason. It was not difficult to become truly angry with
her because she was a most frustrating patient. She
calmly observed his outbursts and waited for them
to subside, and seemed not to profit at all.

He would have ordered her to follow a precise,

hour-by-hour daily schedule of activities in order to structure her time—a regimen which had helped other depressed patients—but he knew she had already done this for herself. She had told him often of "getting through half an hour at a time." He was aware that she had not missed a day at the office, had not neglected her household duties, and had forced herself to appear "normal" to her family and friends.

In truth, she kept herself busy with this surface image and was totally uninvolved in any emotional contact with anyone. Particularly she avoided any real involvement with her therapist, silently keeping to her resolution that she did not need him, and even if she did, she could not trust him. Each time she was tempted to drop her defenses and confide in Dr. Odell, she remembered the unanswered phone call, and she clasped the remembered hurt tighter. She dimly suspected that she was over-reacting but felt too sensitive to chance bringing her pain out into the open.

Only by chance was the unanswered phone call brought into the light of therapy. It was not through any insight on the doctor's part, but rather through happenstance. He found that it was necessary due to a court appearance to change Helen's appointment time and tried to reach her. She did not return his call. As it happened, he did not have to go to Court and she came for her appointment at the regular time and he was there.

As soon as she was settled in her chair he asked her, "Why didn't you return my telephone call yesterday?"

She looked blank for a moment and then said tonelessly, "I did. I tried twice. Your line was busy. I figured if it was important you'd call me back." (It's a one-way street with you, isn't it, Witch Doctor? You sure as hell want your calls returned, but you can completely ignore mine and never even mention why.)

"Yes, I was trying to reach several people yesterday. I thought I was going to have to testify in Court this afternoon, but the hearing was canceled at the last minute. Otherwise I would have called you back." He needled her a little by adding, "Here I thought you were the world's most efficient secretary, too."

Anger flashed in Helen's eyes. "Well, I'll be damned. Am I to understand that you are actually chastising me in some way for not calling you back? You son of a bitch. I'm still waiting for you to return a call to me that I made two months ago.

"What in the hell are you talking about?" he asked, astonished. "What call?"

"What call indeed," she said. "Back at Christmas time, if I am not mistaken, you told me to call you if I felt worse. Any time, you said, any time. Just call and I'll be there, isn't that right? Well, one afternoon when I was barely hanging onto sanity by my eyebrows, I called you. I'm still waiting."

"That's a hell of a thing to do. You've waited so damned long I don't even have a chance to figure out what happened. I don't have the faintest memory of your ever calling me." It was the truth. It was slowly dawning on him that she could have been holding a grudge all this time.

"In other words, you are trying to tell me that it is *my* fault for not returning your call and also *my* fault for your not returning mine." Her woebegone appearance was slowly changing to one of righteous indignation.

"That's right. You said it just about right," he answered, his resentment matching Helen's. "If you didn't go through every day searching for a reason to feel sorry for yourself, we could have straightened this out weeks ago."

"With you around, I don't have to search very far, do I? Every time I come in here you give me something to feel sorry about." (Like paying you my hard earned money for nearly six months to have you side with Steve against me! Or working like a slave at home and at the office and then rushing over here to have you inform me that I am weak!)

"You are unbelievable, you really are," he said shaking his head. "It's getting pretty plain that you've been nursing a quiet grudge over that supposed phone call for weeks."

"*Supposed* phone call! You are a dirty liar! You *know* I made that call. I may have something wrong with my head, but there's nothing wrong with my memory. That's the worst excuse for forgetting something I ever heard." Her voice was now beginning to rise and break with anger.

"I apologize for the word 'supposed,' " Dr. Odell

said. "I do believe that you called. However, I equally believe that somehow I never got the message. But it still makes me mad that you would let this problem cloud every hour for weeks."

"That makes two of us who are mad," she answered, viciously grinding out a cigarette stub and lighting another cigarette. "While we're on the subject of each other's shortcomings — since the hour seems lost today anyhow—there are a few other things you have done that have not particularly endeared you to me." She blew smoke at him fiercely.

Dr. Odell had become aware that Helen's depression had finally disappeared in favor of an angry outburst. Yet he somehow knew that if he withdrew into more of a "therapist's role," the direct exchange of hostility would halt immediately. He was learning that Helen needed an opponent to ventilate anger. He decided to stay in the fight as an involved participant rather than an analyzing observer.

"Don't even bother to tell me. Save it for a few months so you'll really be on safe grounds," he said sardonically.

"Listen, you vulture, it's *my* money we're spending now, and you're stuck with me for twenty more minutes. You can't slam the door and run out to the nearest bar and unburden your troubles to your buddies like Steve does. So you can just listen to it all." She was breathing fast and her chest heaved.

"See! You still haven't told me a thing." He very much wanted to hear her specific complaints, and he wasn't quite sure how to keep the argument at the same angry pitch.

"Well, first of all I still feel mad as hell every time I remember you saying that I was weak. I think that is a damned poor form of treatment—to tell someone who is trying with all their strength to do everything that is required of them—and succeeding, I might add—that she is weak. You damned near convinced me that I was." She paused for breath.

"I don't know exactly what happened in here that afternoon that Steve talked to you," she said hurriedly, "but whatever it was, it wasn't good for me. Every time we have had an argument since, he has used you against me. 'Now, Helen, you're getting overexcited, just like Dr. Odell said you would,' " she mimicked, "or 'Maybe I should call your doctor. You know, I really worry about you when you get so overemotional.' Oh, you've been a great help towards untangling my marriage problems, you have."

Dr. Odell was tempted to stop and interpret her comparison of Steve and himself, but by watching her he could see that she still had a full head of steam. He knew that such an interpretation would cut off the flow of anger immediately, and this he did not want.

"Are you finished?" he asked. "Is it my turn yet?"

"Not yet. I've barely begun. Two things have been bugging hell out of me lately. The first is that I feel all your sympathies are with Steve—not only with Steve, but just general empathies for all the luckless souls who have had the misfortune to come into contact with me. I can actually *feel* you thinking that he is right and I am wrong. But the worst part of it is that you have been able to sit and watch me week after week being miserable. I can stand being miserable far better when there are no witnesses. The combination of your watching me disintegrate and your feeling sympathy for everyone else who had to watch it has made me feel murderous."

"Murderous," he said. "That feeling is so out of character with your downcast mood of the past few weeks that it's hard to believe." He was still trying to keep her spontaneous barrage going.

"That's how much you know, Oh Great Reader of Minds. Perhaps my appearance has been due to the fact that the one I wanted to murder was *myself*! Of course, you wouldn't understand what I'm talking about because you have never felt it. You have been sitting there in your big chair so well-adjusted and smug for so long, you have no inkling what it is to *really* want to die. Maybe you are due for a refresher course. Get out of your ivory tower! Come down and see how all us neurotics live."

"Just about everything you've mentioned, I've been through it personally. I know from experience it's pure hell to feel the way you have been feeling," he told her.

"Then why would you want to torture me?" she asked. "If you *knew* how scared and hopeless I felt, why didn't you call me back that day? It took me hours of revving my motor to get the courage to call and ask you for help. You have no idea how difficult it was for me. Yet you just ignored me. Do you hate me or something? How can you possibly want to help me if you hate me?"

"Helen," he said, "remember? I didn't get that message that you called. I'm telling the truth. Even if you prefer your own version of what happened, keep trying to remember that I really didn't get that call." He was aware that she had believed for so long that he had neglected her, she wouldn't be able to give it up instantly. However, their time together was growing short and he wanted to clarify the phone incident before they parted.

"Perhaps it is too long ago for you to remember what actually happened. Anyway, I agree it is too long ago to argue about now. Truce?" (Whether you're lying or really did forget or didn't get the message makes little difference in the way it made me feel. Anyway, any further discussion about it only wastes my time and my money.)

The doctor felt her offer of a truce was too quick in coming, considering her anger of the moment before. "Now I'm suspicious. You have agreed too quickly and easily. Something tells me that you haven't told me all your thoughts about this."

"I can't be responsible for your suspicious thoughts, can I?" she asked, but now her dimple was beginning to play about her mouth.

"No, but you could help dispel my paranoia a little by telling me why you have halted your anger so quickly."

"Okay. It's because it is wasting too much of my money. Do you realize my hour is nearly over and the whole thing has been a waste? You know, thirty dollars doesn't exactly come so easily to me that I can afford to throw it away arguing with you." (You argued back, too. You ought to chip in fifteen dollars yourself today.)

Before he responded to her, he took special note of the change in her appearance since she arrived. Where she had been dejected, slouched, with eyes downcast, she now sat erect, alert and faced him squarely and almost defiantly.

"Helen," he said, "stop right now and notice how you feel. Without thinking too much about it, tell me what is your state of mind."

She drew her brows together for a moment and then grinned at him. "As a matter of fact, I feel better than I have since the day Steve came in here with me. I still feel a bit angry with you—not the way I did, but more like a hangover just because I am accustomed to it. But my heart wouldn't be in fighting anymore. I think I'd like my husband to take me out to dinner and dancing. It's amazing. One hour ago I was convinced I'd never feel good ever again." She playfully added, "And how do you feel?"

"I'm feeling much better myself. I was getting pretty tired of your long face. You look ten years younger than you did when you arrived—and I feel at least five years younger."

She thought for a moment and said, "It's really

odd. This is the first time in my life I can remember feeling better after being mad as hell. Usually after a fight—particularly with Steve—I just feel worse. I wonder why the difference?"

"Now's the time to figure out the difference, because I think it's important," he said. "You and your husband fight, and it ends up with you feeling depressed. Yet you and I have just had a fight and you're downright cheerful," he observed.

"Damned if I don't feel cheerful, too," she said. "You know, I think it's partly because you didn't stomp out in the middle of it and leave me sputtering. Then, too, you stick to the issues. Steve never sticks to the issues at hand. We start to fight about one thing, and we end up fighting about everything that has happened for the last fifteen years. Now *that* is depressing. By the time we go back into ancient history and rehash all the bitterness we have forgotten what started the current fight."

"Yes, it is important to remember that we had a fight; yet we each survived the other's anger. Do you suppose it makes a difference that I accept you as a sometimes-angry woman?" he asked.

"I think the difference lies in the fact that you accepted me not only as angry but as a bit irrational and accusing. You know, some people—you and Steve, for example—seem to remain somewhat logical even when you are angry. I tend to fly off into orbit and fling out any disconnected unjustifiable recrimination that comes to mind. You ignored my accusa-

tions. Steve always picks up on my actual words and
not my meaning. Maybe that's how we get off on
those tangents."

"I must agree," he said, "you do get a little
carried away."

"It didn't destroy you, did it?" she answered,
smiling.

"No, it didn't," he said. "I'm wondering—do
you still have any impulses to destroy me?"

"Not at the moment, I must admit," she said.
"Of course the true test will come tomorrow morning after I have slept on this whole episode. With me,
the morning after is the acid test." (Actually, old
dear, I like you better and trust you more right now
than I ever have. I just wish I could trust my own
feelings. If I could feel this good toward Steve after a
fight, I'd probably seduce him.) She recrossed her
legs and in so doing her skirt slid a couple of inches
higher on her thighs. She did not pull it back down.

"Okay. For my compulsive nature, let's do a
brief playback of this. You get angry at me; you hold
it in; you get depressed. The depression remains and
even worsens until you express your anger to me
directly. I accept your anger. Actually it doesn't
make much difference whether it's well founded or
irrational. Now we both feel better for it. The only
way you could ruin this is if you get to having second thoughts at home. If you start hashing it over
and begin to think that I, your esteemed therapist,
was faking my acceptance of you in your anger,
you're bound to be depressed again."

"You mean the way I feel after an argument with Steve? Like no matter what the outcome really is, I lose?"

"Right. Even when you win the argument with Steve, you feel that you were wrong and that you are unlovable. Maybe it has been an error on your part to look to Steve for permission to be angry. For whatever reason, he cannot accept your normal, human anger. When it becomes intolerable to him, he stomps out saying, 'You win!' I would guess you'll feel better when you are certain that anger is here to stay and that venting it doesn't do irreparable damage."

"It's a lot to think about. I know I have learned something today, but I'm still not quite sure what it is." She began to gather her cigarettes together and picked up her handbag. "You know, it almost makes me want to go home and pick a fight with Steve to see if I can handle it any better. However," she added, standing, "I simply feel too good to do it. I think I'll stick with my suggestion of having dinner out."

It did not fit into Steve's plans to take his wife out for dinner that night, but she fell asleep immediately upon putting her head on the pillow and slept well. In her dreams she frolicked naked with her therapist. She remembered only a fragment of the dream in the morning, but awoke feeling rested and revived. She did not trust the sensation to last but expected the familiar feelings of foreboding to descend at any moment. It was with feelings of gratefulness that she made it through the entire day with her newfound peace still intact.

Chapter 12

When Helen's mood of optimism remained steady for several weeks and she repeatedly demonstrated that she could express anger more openly, Dr. Odell made his decision to put her on the couch. This decision was based on the fact that once Helen's depression had lifted and she no longer had frequent anxiety attacks, her motivation to focus on her inner feelings greatly diminished. She consistently arrived later for her appointments, categorically refused to be serious, and made every attempt to turn her therapy sessions into social events. They both enjoyed these "tea parties," but Dr. Odell knew that she had to dig deeper and explore her feelings in more depth before she could be safe from future recurrence of anxiety and depression. Helen, in contrast, felt that her new state of well-being precluded discussing her previous terrible days for fear they might return.

Although the doctor used the couch with constantly decreasing frequency with his patients, he thought Helen needed the special conditions provided by the couch to facilitate her focusing on her inner feelings. He hoped that the status of being more "alone" with her feelings—without being able to read his facial expression and react to it—and the general lack of emotional interchange would bring about the release of unconscious material she had heretofore omitted.

Helen's three months on the couch was a dismal experience for both of them. Each week her tears began the moment her head hit the couch, but she was never able to define the source of the tears either to herself or to the doctor. While Dr. Odell did confirm that Helen had an incapacitating dependency problem, he also learned that the use of the couch was inexplicably unsuccessful for Helen. In June he had her resume her sessions in the chair.

It was during this period also that Dr. Odell brought the blackboard on which he chalked up the number of minutes Helen was late each time and the dollar value thereof. He didn't discuss the blackboard with her, but silently recorded her wasted time and money weekly as she watched. Each week Helen became more infuriated as she fumbled for excuses to refuse the uncompromising blackboard. When the blackboard amount hit $100, she delivered a scathing speech to Dr. Odell accusing him of being a calculator, but she did begin to arrive on time.

Helen's relief at being back in the chair was evident. Her depression had not returned, and she felt and looked better than she had for several months. Her manner became breezier and her sense of humor returned. She still tended to discuss the here-and-now in her therapy and was quite unable to relate her feelings to events in the past.

In the middle of July she arrived, breathless but punctual, for her five o'clock appointment. Dr. Odell immediately noticed a subtle change in her but could not quite put his finger on just what it was.

"My God, it must be 130 degrees out there," she said, flinging herself into her chair. She kicked off her shoes, stretched her legs full length and wiggled her toes luxuriously. Dr. Odell noticed she was not wearing stockings. His glance moved upward and he decided she was not wearing a bra either.

"Even allowing for your exaggerations, I suppose it is hotter than hell," he said. "You look pretty good under the circumstances though."

"Thank you, kind sir." She smiled, and lifted her long dark hair off her neck with her hand. "Your air conditioned office is very inviting today." He became aware that her hair was loose around her shoulders today, as if she had removed all the pins. It made her look less businesslike than he had ever seen her. She began the mad search in her huge bag for cigarettes and matches, and as the air stirred around her, he noticed that she was wearing perfume.

"Hmmmm, you even smell good today," he said. Almost at the same time that he intellectually added up the data, he felt a strong male interest in her. He was inexplicably reminded of a sexy, young girl he had dated in his first year of college.

"Just my own natural fragrant body," she smiled

displaying her dimples, "with a bit of help from Revlon." (I noticed that look. It's nice to be treated as a woman rather than as a sick patient.)

"You seem a little different today—sort of like party-party. Anything special going on today?" The invitation to let him in on the "something special" included either activities or thoughts or both. His intent was to inquire as to how aware she was of her own sexuality without making her so self-conscious that she became defensive.

"As a matter of fact, dear doctor, today I am not a working girl. Having worked late two nights for my slave driving boss on a rush case, he gave me the afternoon off. I have been lying in the sun beside a neighbor's pool, sipping Margueritas and having a ladylike discussion about sex." (Well, Doctor, now I've said the dirty word. I have opened new vistas for you to explore. Take advantage—I have the false courage of two Margueritas in me today to take the plunge into the Forbidden Subject.)

"You do look a little turned on," he said. "Was it a male or a female neighbor?"

"Alas, 'twas a female. As you know from experience, it's difficult for me to bring up the subject with the opposite sex."

She wiggled a bit uncomfortably in her chair. Dr. Odell could not tell if the high color in her cheeks was a sunburn or if she was blushing.

"I have felt like leering at you today. Is it just the dirty old man in me, or is something going on today?" She seemed to be saying that she needed some support, and he chose to help her out by admitting to his own sexual feelings first.

"I don't know what you mean by 'going on.' If it is, it's only in my head." She crossed her arms over her chest, and the gesture had the opposite effect from what she wanted because it made her lack of a brassiere even more obvious. She giggled. "I suddenly have the impulse to convince you I am a virgin," she said and giggled again.

"That's a pretty wicked sounding laugh for a virgin," he said.

"I read lusty books," she said, still looking flustered. (My God, what was I thinking of, coming here today without any underwear on! I'll never take another drink.)

"You know, I'll permit you to have feelings towards me that you don't have to do anything about," he said.

"Who said the feelings were about you? Now you are assuming. You are supposed to be a scientific man and scientists never assume anything." Now she pulled her feet back toward her and crossed her ankles. (This has gotten out of hand. Suppose I should admit my feelings are toward him? Who can tell where it would go, here alone in this dark room—with that couch!) She looked at her watch and recrossed her arms across her breasts, her face crimson.

"When you start arguing like a lawyer, it makes me doubly suspicious. Then again maybe I am flattering myself, and your bare legs and your perfume and your sexy dress are meant for someone else today."

He knew he was nailing her down with the evidence on hand. On the other hand, he was freeing her to deny seductive behavior toward him specifically if she could not tolerate such an admission.

"Okay, you win. I confess. I rigged myself specially for you today —but not with any evil designs to have my way with you," she said. "Somehow it hasn't gone quite right though. Now I'm embarrassed and I'm curling my toes so hard I'm getting cramps in my legs, and if I had on a sash, I'm sure I'd be twisting it." (I wish I were an oyster and could pull into a shell.)

"Well, Helen," he answered, "you've always looked pretty sexy to me anyway, so your special efforts weren't needed very much."

She looked mildly astonished. "You're kidding! I always felt as if you were so intent on what goes on in my head, you probably didn't even realize I'm a female." (That has got to be some kind of doctor-patient line of his. He is so totally controlled and cool and collected, I can't even imagine him having a sexy thought about a patient.)

"I suppose you would be happier if I would leer a little more obviously."

"No, actually I think I liked it better when I was firm in my belief that you saw me as a neuter. Somehow discussing sex with you makes me quite uncomfortable. Actually, what would make me happier is if Steve would take to leering at me a bit more."

"Right now I can't do anything about Steve," Dr. Odell said, "but maybe we can do something about you. You do seem to feel awkward and self-conscious enough that we ought to talk about it."

"It'll only make it worse," she answered. (I don't know if it is the drinks or the subject matter of this conversation, but I must get out of here soon or I will actually make an advance toward him.) She blushed again and curled her toes until the muscles in her calves ached.

"Are you curling your toes again?" he asked to call her attention to her own feelings.

"Yes," she answered, smiling. "Now every time I do it you'll know I'm having sexy thoughts, won't you?"

"Yes, but you do seem to have a lot of static along with them. Tell me about some of those uncomfortable feelings."

"I feel as if I'm bringing up an unmentionable topic—sort of the way I used to when I brought up tales of blood and gore at the dinner table. Isn't that ridiculous? Here I am thirty-five years old, married, and have two children, and I'm embarrassed to tears at discussing sex with you. I mean I could tell you a couple of dirty stories and it wouldn't bother me. But to sit down seriously and discuss my *own* feelings and my *own* sexual life—that's a different matter entirely."

"Your background sounds about like mine." He noticed her visibly relax at this pronouncement. "But let's dwell on yours. How did your family handle feelings like this?"

"They ignored them as far as I can tell. I've even

tried to imagine my mother and father in bed, but I simply can't. My mother never, never told me anything about sex. However, she used to read aloud every item in the paper about rapes and sex crimes, and then cluck her tongue and say she didn't know what the country was coming to. I never could quite fit together her denial of sex on the one hand and her avid appetite for the lurid details in the newspaper on the other."

"You mean your mother was both attracted to and repelled by sex?" he inquired.

"Exactly. Repelled by her own feelings but terribly attracted to those of the general public, I guess," she said.

"It's kind of hard to believe she really didn't tell you something about sex or masturbation or something."

"Well, she did explain menstruation to me. So at least *that* wasn't a surprise. But somehow our communication broke down at that point." She thought for a moment and added, "I suppose she did that in self-defense. I was so horrified as a child at the sight of blood, I guess she felt that if she didn't forewarn me I would become hysterical or cause a family scandal when it happened."

"Did it go all right then when you started menstruating?"

It must have, because I can't remember any traumatic feelings. You are asking me to remember an awfully long time back now," she answered. "As a matter of fact, I remember feeling a secret pride at

being truly a grown-up woman. So I'd say it must
have been handled okay."

"How old were you when your periods began?"
he asked, hoping to draw her out more about this
phase of her life.

"I was the wise old age of eleven. I was only
in the sixth grade and I do remember I was well ahead
of most of my friends."

"Did you discuss sex with your friends?"

"Only in the most general way with girl friends.
We were terribly curious about the whole topic. None
of our mothers seemed to be able to give us any but
the most perfunctory information," she answered. "I
do remember the first time I experienced honest-to-
goodness sexy feelings. I must have been about thirteen or fourteen—barely in high school—and one of
those vividly pornographic mimeographed stories
was furtively passed around school. It was entitled
"The Nubian Slave" as I recall. In detailed and graphic
language it described a male slave being chained down
while a series of young, especially trained virgins
performed various erotic acts upon him, ending in
the most vivid and explicit accounts you could imagine. It had a sensational effect on me. I didn't really
feel there was anyone I could discuss it with, but I do
remember feeling both excited and a bit upset because I couldn't quite define my excitement. Who in
the world writes those things anyway?" This entire
recitation was told with her eyes downcast.

"I don't know, but I do remember reading the
same thing about the same age, so it must have made

the rounds. It certainly did turn me on, too," he said.

"I suppose that's the definition I would use to-day, too," she said. "At the time I simply felt be-wildered by the degree of my feelings but I couldn't put a name on them."

"Did you discuss these feelings with anyone?"

"With you today," she answered. "It's the first time."

"Talking about sex seems more forbidden to you than having sex," he said. "To get dead serious, why is sex such an embarrassing topic for you?"

"I wince when you say 'dead serious.' Somehow it takes on ominous overtones. And anyway, I don't think it's so damned unusual—I mean, normal ordin-ary people don't run around talking about their sex life as a routine part of the day. I don't think that my embarrassment makes me sick or neurotic. Just re-member, your line of work deals daily with this sort of thing, and you're accustomed to probing around in everyone else's libido. I wonder how open and expan-sive you'd be if I suddenly began quizzing *you* about whether or not you were feeling horny. Then I could be the calm questioner and you could curl *your* toes." She smiled with satisfaction.

"You have now given a brilliant defense, Coun-selor, but you have once again evaded giving a reason for your own discomfort in talking about sex. Re-member, you had the same feelings before I ever came along."

"Well, then, that certainly shoots your theory full of holes that they are directed toward you, doesn't it?" she asked. (I would give my right arm if I had on a girdle and a bra—and a chastity belt!)

"Even if you hadn't told me, I would suspect that you work for a lawyer. You probably know very well that I was referring not to your sexual feelings but to your embarrassment and awkwardness."

"Well, now you've done it. If I did have sexual feelings when I came in here today your clinical dissection of them—analysis if you will—has totally destroyed them. It has also destroyed the lovely glow that I spent all afternoon to get. And my reward is being told that I am awkward." (Awkward! Clumsy! Sexless! I should have known that is the way he sees me. Maybe that's the way Steve sees me too — it certainly is the way he treats me.)

"You're doing it again, Helen. You're diverting away from the main topic by trying to start a fight with me. I'm feeling very patient, so try again."

"I don't know what you want from me. To admit that I'm embarrassed? Well, I've admitted that. I don't know why. You tell me."

"I'm not exactly sure either, but I keep thinking about the word 'childish.' From my own experience lots of people stay away from their childlike feelings at any cost. Most of us have a picture in our minds of ourselves as adult that may even be super-adult. Anything that detracts from this self-image we tend to disclaim. You are sounding like a super-adult who can't admit to the more childlike feelings of embarrassment and self-consciousness about the adult subject of sex."

"Go on, Professor," she said sarcastically but evidencing genuine interest.

"I am reminded of when I was a graduate student in therapy with my psychology professor. I felt as if I should know all about sex. I couldn't bear to bring up anything that implied that I was other than a highly sophisticated, experienced psychologist and man of the world. He didn't realize my feelings and we never got off the ground. I don't want that to happen to you and me. It sounds as if you have never really had anyone whom you could frankly discuss sex with."

"That isn't exactly true either," Helen said. "I just told you I had a discussion on this very subject this afternoon with a neighbor by her pool. I also have several sophisticated friends—one in particular who is a rather gay divorcee—and she and I talk about it endlessly. The difference is we are discussing *her* sex life and her many affairs. I can assure you that under those circumstances I appear to be very worldly and unshockable."

"How about Steve?" he asked. "Do you and he ever discuss sex?"

"Good God, no. I don't think the subject has ever been brought up for discussion between us. If you think I am embarrassed, try to talk to him openly about the activities in the bedroom."

Dr. Odell remembered his brief encounter with Steve and Steve's sheepish smile and high-school-boy attitude. He felt that for once Helen probably wasn't exaggerating.

"Yes," the doctor answered, "I recall his expression when I brought up the topic of your sexual relations with him. You mean he can perform but he can't talk."

"Even the performance has deteriorated lately. The trouble seems to date back to the beginning of my 'scares' or to the beginning of my therapy. The two were so close together, I don't know which one affected us most."

Dr. Odell recalled Steve's saying to him that "Helen usually takes very good care of me, but she doesn't seem to be very interested in it since her emotional troubles started."

"As I recall," he said, "Steve thought you had lost interest when you began to have your anxiety attacks." Thinking about this, Dr. Odell studied Helen again, and decided she looked like a very sexy woman. It was hard to believe she could be cold and frigid.

"If that were true, I would have recovered when the attacks disappeared. Recovered I am not. It isn't that I give the standard excuse that I am tired or that I have a headache. It's more as if we avoid each other entirely. If Steve goes to bed early, I stay up and watch the late show. If I go to bed early, Steve goes over and hangs around the Skull n' Crossbones with his buddies drinking beer. We are seldom awake in bed together. When we are, for the most part we carefully avoid touching each other. Hurrah for king-size beds." (In other words, I am disappointed and unlaid —and rather horny. At least I was horny until I got here and you began to dissect me. I wonder if you are this clinical with your wife.)

"What feelings have come about since this began?" he asked, hoping to get some kind of emotional response rather than bare facts about her sexual life.

"Mixed, very mixed," she answered. "Sometimes I lie in bed and wait for Steve to come in, hoping he will. He rarely does and then I feel castaway and undesirable. On the other hand, on the few occasions he does come in, I invariably pretend to be asleep or I get engrossed in a book to avoid him. I'm quite a difficult one to make happy, wouldn't you say?"

"I could think of some uncomplimentary names for you, but I have a hunch you have oversimplified the situation. You seem to be taking the entire responsibility."

"Oh, that I do, that I do," she said too readily. "When the budget is in the red, it is my fault because I have made the budget my responsibility. When the children are naughty or when they have to be driven to appointments, it is my responsibility because I have taken on their discipline and their schedules as my own obligations. Therefore, I suppose that somehow I must have set myself up to be responsible for our bedroom schedule and when that disintegrates, it must be totally my fault."

"In words, you are taking the responsibility, but in tone of voice you are laying it on Steve pretty heavily," he remarked.

"Well, I'll tell you something, my learned friend, I think the most complimentary act Steve could perform would be to come home and throw me on the bed, slap me around a bit if I resisted, ravish me, and then pound his chest like a beast and take the entire responsibility," she said emphatically. "I'll give you a further bit of information. If I suggested that he do such a thing, he wouldn't come home from the Skull n' Crossbones for a week!"

Dr. Odell threw back his head and laughed aloud. "Any girl that can fantasy a scene like that can't be all bad—or maybe I should say good." He chuckled again. He was aware that he felt sexually aroused. He felt it was a shame to waste such a sexy woman on a man who preferred being mothered.

"I know that about an hour after I leave here, I shall have the perfect answer to that remark. I always do, you know. Sometimes as I drive home I think of exactly what I should have said to you when you said thus and so. I think tonight when the perfect response comes to me, I'll send it in a letter so as not to lose it." Her tone of voice did not imply that she was truly angry but that she was having doubts about how he felt.

Now Dr. Odell roared with laughter. "I'd better explain myself," he said. "In the first place, just looking at you, it's rather difficult to take you seriously about any extreme sexual problem. In the second place, I was not laughing at your sexual dilemma which I recognize as being painful. But your colorful description of your 'rape fantasy' had some real appeal for me."

She blushed again. "My hour is over," she said,

glancing at her watch. "I might add that I am not too unhappy to notice it either," she said, but she was smiling.

"Let me summarize this hour so that it might make more sense to both of us."

"If you can stand it, so can I."

"Notice that we really did start to talk about that important subject, sex. And we have both survived. I have learned that you have been raised even more puritanically than I and that it causes you a great deal of embarrassment to talk about your sexual feelings and behavior.

"Don't forget," he said, "even though we only touched on the subject, I know that it took some real courage on your part to begin."

"Don't forget the two Margueritas either," she said.

"Don't try to give the credit to the Margueritas," he said. "Bring up the topic of sex someday. Don't give up on it."

"That's a fair enough offer," she said. (I wonder if I can get out of here without bouncing in front and jiggling behind.)

She rose and moved stiffly out of the room. Dr. Odell noticed she was walking very carefully, as if she were balancing a book on her head.

CHAPTER 13

A few days later Helen kept her word and Dr. Odell received the first of many of her letters. The doctor was not aware at that time, but her letters were to become an integral part of her therapy. In her writings to Dr. Odell, she was particularly able to express her feelings toward him with an ease she never achieved during her hours.

June 25

Dear Dr. Odell:

I would not be writing you this letter if I thought I would ever be able to say these things to you in your office. When I am there with you, I feel that you out-maneuver and bully me. I do not like that feeling! It is as if each time I enter your Inner Sanctum—weaponless—you back me into the corner and mentally slap me around a few times and send me on my merry way a little stunned.

I can come up with very logical answers to your probing and leading questions on the way home from my sessions, but all I can do while I am there is grope around wildly for a safe, comfortable subject, irrele-

vant though it may sometimes be. I have the impulse to throw my shoe at you when you drag me unwillingly back to the subject at hand and when you sit there so damned calm and composed and pleased with yourself. I suppose it would be a bit unsettling to me also, however, should you suddenly come unglued and wring your hands and wail.

I have been quite peeved with you since my last appointment. I do not feel that you really took me seriously when I told you that I hated the idea of sex. It just so happens that it took me about three weeks to bring up this subject and to tell you about it, and for my valiant efforts I was not even taken seriously. Now, that is my trick and I do not want you to begin joking about serious things. Maybe you could write a little paper for one of the journals and entitle it "Frigidity Can Be Fun" or "How to be Gay and Carefree Sans Sex."

Perhaps if you think this is so funny, I can manage to break my leg or break out in hives and send you into peals of laughter. Sometimes, you know, subjects that may be amusing when viewed objectively take on a different aspect when viewed subjectively.

I do not intend ever to discuss the subject of sex again—only to tell you that it would not be taken so light-heartedly if it should happen to you.

That's enough for today. I don't want to take you from your cauldron and hot coals for too long a time. You may now get back to making some other poor patient anxious and fearful.

H. James

Dr. Odell never felt very successful in his attempts to get Helen to entirely take responsibility for
the feelings and ideas expressed in her own letters.
She behaved as though she might or might not have
authored them. Sometimes he ignored the fact that he
had received a letter; she ignored it, too. Occasionally
he would read a paragraph to her from one of them;
she listened politely as if it had nothing to do with her.
If he incidentally quoted part of one to her, she either
expressed guilt for having taken up so much of his
time having to read it or vaguely suggested that she
had not really been herself when she wrote it. But
the letters continued to come.

July 8

Dear. Dr. Odell:

*I felt last week again that "something is wrong
in Therapyville." I can never exactly put my finger
on just what goes "right" or "wrong" in my appointments, but I know after I leave which way the session
went. Last time it went wrong. I think I have the idea
that if I do not come to see you and demonstrate
anxiety and agitation and tears that you will think I
am well, and you will "fire" me. Therefore, it follows
that I do not dare get too well, or I will not have a
doctor if I get "sick" again.*

*I was so angry with you when I left last time, if
I could have found anyone willing to be my second, I
would have challenged you to a duel. I thought about
everything you had said on the way home and I did
not like one word of it. You know, it just could be*

that you don't like women! I would love to see a copy of your Rorschach protocols—I'll bet they are just full of witches. I'll bet your mother let you cry when you were hungry.

You are always screaming at me for jumping in and taking responsibility all over the place—at home, at the office—everywhere. You imply that I am a controlling bitch.

I have told you several times that I do not like myself very much these days, and you make me feel as if I certainly have good reason. My best idea yet is to join the Peace Corps and go teach the Chinese how to play the bongo drums—except maybe for the Chinese.

Anyone who would drive across Phoenix in the middle of the summer in the five o'clock traffic like a fire-eating dragon to listen for one hour to ungentle- manly questions and painful "interpretations" ought to have one's head examined!

H. James

July 29

Dear Doctor Odell:

I considered writing to you last night, but I got too busy trying to find a blackboard and chalk to put up over Steve's and my bed. I figure that if your theory is correct regarding my competitiveness, there ought to be some way to keep score.

You have no idea how difficult it was for me to tell you about that sexy dream I had about you. I must say I did not like your reaction to my recitation. I am going to exercise iron control over all my dreams in the future, and I never intend to have another which will embarrass me to tell you. Furthermore, I don't intend to let you get into any of them and if you should, I would appreciate it if you would try to behave yourself.

I do seem to have difficulties in my relationship with you. I wish I could think of you as a passive neuter to whom I pay money to listen to my trivial problems. I wish I could say to myself, "It's my money and if I want to go see him and spend an hour weeping and wringing my hands and whining, that's my privilege." But I can't do that. My last very wet session was Pure Hell when I came apart in front of you. It makes me wonder where therapy leaves off and self-pity begins. When I weep and sniffle in front of you I feel that I have automatically depreciated in your eyes in direct ratio to the amount that I have depreciated in my own.

I sometimes feel that therapy is some sort of diabolical endurance test or obstacle course to which there is no reason or sense. It's like being sent into battle without any weapon and being confused because I am defeated. And I am a volunteer, to boot.

                                                  H. James

                                        August 7
Dear Dr. Odell:

I have been thinking about your definition of "transference." If I understand you correctly, all these feelings I have toward you aren't really toward you at all. They are actually just warmed-up leftovers of feel-

ings I had toward someone else that got misplaced. Now I am attributing them to you and getting angry when I should be mad as hell at Aunt Sophie for spanking me when I was three. It doesn't make much sense, but I will accept it only because of your impressive credentials.

But I will sure as hell tell you how it makes me feel. It makes me feel like your average, run-of-the-mill psychiatric patient. I hate having to admit being a patient in the first place and I really hate it when I think that you are thinking: Hmmm, I think it's time to push her into discussing her feelings about me. How dull and boring. Just another patient with the same old feelings and problems. Tra la la, life is monotonous. Why, Helen James is just like Such and Such, and the answer to her problem was So and So. I think I can find that on page 205." That is how I feel that you think about me! And I do not like it.

However, if your description to me of transference is correct, I just want you to know I am fully aware that I would be struggling with these same feelings about you if you were ninety years old, had a long gray beard, a pot belly and gravy down your shirt.

H. James

August 19

Dear Dr. Odell:

I don't know why, but I seem to feel the need after my session with you to summarize my feelings on good, solid paper. Somehow they don't seem so intangible and floating then.

I certainly did not like my hour yesterday. I cringe every time I think about it. I find myself at odd moments gathering my defenses against the barrage next week. In the past I have even found myself quite consciously cutting off fantasies about you—not because they, in themselves, are unpleasant or disturbing to me, but because I am afraid you will ask me about them and I don't want to have anything to tell. When I try to discuss my private daydreams with you, it makes me feel like a chart or a number. It infuriates me that I should have such common feelings in the first place. And I think it will always and forever be painful and humiliating for me to discuss them with you.

Perhaps I will paint a picture on the new canvas Steve gave me for my birthday and entitle it "Patient's View of Therapy"—Salvador Dali style—with nails being driven into a head which is held with a vice— and a nice bluish-green face with little drops of blood here and there. I doubt that it would be very serene for hanging on the wall of the drawing room, but perhaps I could sell it to one of the drug companies for use in advertising tranquilizers.

The above is a letter from a completely healthy and cured patient—just loaded with wisdom and health. Where does one apply for Medicare???

H. James

August 23

Dear Doctor Odell:

I hate this part of the year. When it is August in Phoenix, the best place to be is elsewhere. I even find myself envying the children while they are at camp this week in the mountains.

I miss the kids terribly. The house seems too quiet and empty without them. I can hardly bear to go into their bedrooms. If there had been some way to pluck that plane back out of the air on Sunday when they took off, I would have done so. They looked so little to me getting on that big plane by themselves —and so damned competent. They waved good-by as if they were going to a friend's house for an hour.

I guess I never tell you very much about my children. I suppose that is because this is an area where I don't have much trouble. I am convinced that I have the brightest, best behaved, most lovable children who ever lived. Brag, brag, brag.

I guess the same is true about Steve. Not that he is so lovable and well behaved, but that I don't tell you much about him. There seems so little to tell. He goes to the office and he comes home. We don't talk much. If we do, we argue. There you have it in a nutshell.

Do you remember several months back when you asked me to describe my marriage? I have thought back since then to my description. Given an hour and asked to describe a marriage, naturally every married person in the world would have a different story to tell. But, don't you agree that if you have been married to someone for a third of your life you might find something good to say? I honestly can't remember saying one good thing about my marriage, and this is most distressing to me. At the time I was talking to you, I felt that I was being honest and fairly descriptive in my story of my wedded life. Somehow it all came out to be a story of bitching about money and the various jobs I have had. Not one word about tenderness or love—or any of the other words usually associated with my chosen subject of the day. I remember at the end of that session feeling like a fink who had just "ratted" on someone.

I feel very mixed up tonight. I started out writing this letter, I think, because I was lonely for the children. When I am lonely, as you know, I often write to you—or just write, period, and call it a "letter" and send it off to you.

Now that I have written it, I feel worse than when I started. I am more lonely. I think I am lonely for the way I used to feel about my marriage—in the early years. Hopeful. Lonely for hopefulness. God, that sounds like a B movie. I don't even know what I am lonely for.

Do you remember in one of Thomas Wolfe's novels—Look Homeward, Angel I think it was—he said something like: "Four thousand years ago in Crete you can find the beginning of the love which ended yesterday in Texas." It makes my problems seem small and less significant. I like that. I like Thomas Wolfe. I would also like to blame all my feelings now on some 4,000-year-old Cretan. I sometimes wish the hell I were in Crete!

I will be glad to see you again. Sometimes these few days between sessions seem very long.

Helen

September 3

Dear Doctor Odell:

I have been in this routine with you for nearly a year now. Sometimes I wonder if I have made any progress at all. I don't mean to say that you haven't helped me. I truly don't have "scares" anymore, and seem able to chase it away when I feel one approaching. However, I don't seem to have any more idea now than I did a year ago what caused them in the first place. Nor do I have any certainty that they are gone never to return. So I suppose I'll just keep coming to you month after month until you tell me yourself it is time to leave.

I have been trying to decide whether we had another "tea party" yesterday when I was there. I had that familiar feeling on the way home that I might as well have struck up a conversation with the milkman for all that I told you. I don't seem to be able to bring up much relevant material unless I am upset, do I? I suppose you will tell me next time whether or not it was a "tea party." In the meantime, I will try to work up a nervous tic and tremor or throw a little fit for you in order to make the hour seem worthwhile.

Actually I have no idea why I am writing to you tonight. I don't feel the least upset. You don't suppose I am actually becoming dependent upon my relationship with you in some way? The truth is I am writing to you only because if I stop you might take to reading "Dear Abby" and it would warp your mind.

Helen

September 13

Dear Doctor Odell:

    I had thought I would be an oriented parent the next time I wrote to you, but it turns out that I am still disoriented as yet. I dashed madly home from your office tonight because I thought there was a "Parent Orientation Meeting" at school tonight—only to learn that it is next week. Oh, well, what can you expect from a mental patient?

    It is perfectly lovely to have the children home again and settled in school. It is also—thanks to you —quite marvelous to wake up in the morning and not experience those feelings of dread and doom which were so much a part of me a year ago. I would not want to live last September over again.

    Steve seems more aware of me lately. Perhaps my happier outlook these days is contagious. He has been staying home every night. Most often we just watch TV, but occasionally we actually talk. There is a nasty side of me that wonders if all it means is he is mad at the bartender of the Skull n' Crossbones. I wonder why it is so hard for me to give him any credit?

    I know that I have done this with you, too— failed to give credit when it was due. Often when I have felt relief or even elation after an hour with you, I have told myself, "It certainly isn't because of him! It is probably just that my glands have been acting up and finally gotten back into production, and I would have felt fine whether I saw Dr. Odell or not." On the other hand, when I leave your office absolutely miserable and looking as if I had spent a week at the

Wailing Wall, I never fail to think, "It's all because of that damned Dr. Odell and his sadistic, accusing attitude that has made me so miserable." I am beginning to see myself as a person who is able to give credit to others only for the bad and not for the good.

For some reason my realization that I have done this with you—taken away credit when it was due and blamed you for feelings that were not your fault —makes it clearer to me that I have done it with others many times. Not only Steve, but my parents, too. My achievements have been mine alone; my failures have been partially theirs.

Do you think eventually I might be able to apply other therapy lessons to my daily life? My God, is that what therapy is all about? I do believe I see a glimmer of light at the end of the long dark hallway.

Helen

Helen's letters to Dr. Odell particularly illustrated her basic difficulty in trusting anyone. While she softened her feelings of distrust with occasional masochistic humor, her problems with dependency and trust were threads which were woven through each letter. She could not give up the desire for closeness but could not tolerate the fear of being hurt or rejected. She existed in a constant state of loneliness, never permitting herself to relate closely enough to anyone so she could be hurt by his opinion. She was overprepared for criticism, and tried to keep herself in a position with others where she could reject before being rejected.

She once admitted to Dr. Odell she was always

surprised when he was there for her appointment. It mattered not that she faithfully kept her own appointments, nor did it matter that he had always been there on time when she arrived. She nonetheless was primed each time she came to find his door locked or a note on it telling her to go away. The mere repetition of favorable experience did not seem to affect her negative expectations at all.

Helen's letters abruptly ceased in mid-September. She gave no more explanation for their discontinuance than she did for their beginning. However, she began to speak more freely in their hours together about her feelings toward Dr. Odell; it no longer seemed necessary to her to write what she could not say. Dr. Odell's acceptance of her letters had made the need for her to write them obsolete. Somehow in her mind, his acceptance of her letters was also an acceptance of her.

The two of them later did discuss this "letter period" of her therapy. Helen admitted that Dr. Odell's tolerance of them—his encouragement actually—had made her feel "special." She also admitted that while she felt guilty for taking up his time to read them, for which he never charged her, she didn't feel guilty enough to quit doing it.

To himself Dr. Odell had partially explained her underlying motivation for the letter writing. He felt that the letters represented a hidden way for Helen to get "more than the other kids." Not only did he give her his time and thoughts when she was present for her session; he had to give her his time and thoughts when he read her letters. It is pretty difficult to read a letter from someone and not think about her. It became a way for Helen to feel loved, while basically still denying her own competitiveness and need for love.

Helen's letters made it obvious to Dr. Odell, in terms of her transference, that she expected him to be as rejecting of her competitiveness and need for love as had the parental figures in her past. By accepting and reading her letters, he was able to give her love without either of them mentioning it, and in this way she was able to accept affection from him.

When the letters ceased and Helen began to express herself more openly in their hours together, she began to truly grow up. She was no longer fearful or embarrassed about expressing her childlike feelings. It was no longer so difficult to openly seek his approval or admit that she needed it. She gradually became able to describe her fantasies about him. Only in the area of sexual feelings did she occasionally still blush and threaten to "resume my letters again because sex is still an embarrassing subject more easily written about than spoken about—even more easily done than spoken about.

They were now able to laugh together and relate as two adults—and sometimes as two children.

CHAPTER 14

By the holiday season Helen's punctuality was no longer noteworthy, for she had been on time since the episode of the blackboard. However, it was still a rare occasion when she arrived early enough to sit quietly and relax for a few minutes before Dr. Odell summoned her from the waiting room into his office.

On the day of her last session before Christmas, he was pleasantly surprised to find her settled snugly into an armchair obviously engrossed in a hardback copy of *Portnoy's Complaint*. In fact, she was so absorbed in her reading she did not look up when he came to greet her.

She was wearing a red wool dress with a bright gold Christmas pin, her only jewelry. It was a simple dress, long sleeved and high necked, but gave the effect of festivity. She obviously had taken pains with her grooming today. Dr. Odell noticed that there were several gaily wrapped packages at her feet. He was feeling considerable curiosity as he said for the second time, "Helen, won't you come in?"

She looked up from her book and smiled. "I'm trying to decide between you and Philip Roth."

Do you realize this is the first time I have seen you reading since your first appointment?" he said. "When you get this relaxed, I predict you won't need my services much longer."

"I'll bet you didn't even know I was literate," she said. "And don't worry—I'll be around for a while. Why don't you be helpful and carry a couple of these packages in. I'm giving you a Christmas party today."

Dr. Odell picked up two gift wrapped packages from the floor while Helen carried a large cardboard carton filled with ice in which was nestled a bottle of champagne. Feeling a bit cautious about the situation, he followed her into the office and closed the door.

Helen calmly took her accustomed place in the chair and lifted the cover from one of the boxes. From its tissue-filled interior she brought out two crystal champagne glasses. She handed them to the doctor, saying, "You may pour, sir."

Dr. Odell expertly popped the cork from the bottle and poured two glasses of champagne commenting, "This looks like the kind of therapy hour I've always hoped for but never actually had. I'd like to propose a toast, but my curiosity wins out first. What's the occasion?"

Helen held her glass to the doctor's and said,

"I'll propose the toast and then I will be happy to enlighten you on my motivation." She raised her glass. "To an absence of 'scares.'"

"I'll drink to that—and also to your absolute trust in me," he added, slightly tongue-in-cheek. They sipped the champagne.

"Just what I was thinking about," Helen answered. "I know you find this difficult to believe, but I truly do trust you more than I have anyone in my life. But not enough, I admit. I'm still ready to endow you with unflattering qualities at the drop of a pin, as you may have noticed."

She smiled at him and sipped from her glass again. "Actually that brings us to part of the reason for your party today. You see, I do have a partially ulterior motive. Not entirely though. For one thing, I just felt happy today comparing how I feel now with how I felt last year at this time. I thought I would never get through the holiday season a year ago, feeling so miserable while the world expected me to feel jolly and festive. That's one reason for the bubbly today."

She wrinkled her brow and thought for a moment. "My ulterior motive is that—I don't exactly know how to phrase it—I guess I have always wondered if I couldn't talk to you more easily on a person-person basis rather than one of doctor-patient. So today I am arranging a social situation to see if it helps. So far I think it does. Now I'm wondering how I can afford to bring champagne each week and still pay you for my therapy, too. Of course, if we are only social friends, I needn't pay you at all, what do you think?" She looked teasingly at him over her glass. (If you really cared about me, you wouldn't charge me.)

"Okay. No more fees. Just bring a bottle of champagne with you each week. How does that sound?" He decided to play her game with her and knew that this was a perfectly safe offer to make.

"Very compromising, Doctor, that's how it sounds. I would be forever wondering what you were going to collect and when." (That thought doesn't make me as uneasy as it should—or as it once did. Still I'm glad I wore underwear today. I wonder if he remembers the day I didn't. God! What an awful memory *that* day stirs up.)

He laughed. "From the way you look today in that red dress, I have all sorts of ideas of what I might try to collect. But I suspect you still need a therapist more than a lover."

"Try me," she answered. "On second thought, don't. I simply can't go through all this again with a new therapist so I suppose you are destined to remain in that role yourself. I must admit, though, the idea is appealing to me. And there are times I'm not so sure I need a therapist more than a lover." (I wish you could be both.)

"Especially after champagne, I feel that, for today only, I would rather be a lover than a therapist."

"That's the first thing you've said that made me a little nervous. It makes me think you let your fantasies run away with you. Suddenly I want to control your fantasies. I'm not sure in which direction. I'm doing it again—being unfeminine and aggressive—admitting to another wish to control."

"There you go again, Helen. Interrupting a perfectly good social hour with therapy. Do you wish me to comment on that last remark?"

"Please do. Since I'm to go on paying my fee, I want to get my money's worth," she smiled.

He poured them each another glass of champagne before commenting.

"Now you sound like a patient again."

"Well, that's not so bad, is it?" she replied.

"It's not so bad for me, but I remember when you thought of being a patient as the most lowly form of human existence."

"That is but one sign of my tremendous improvement, don't you think? You will know I am perfectly healthy and well adjusted when I carry a sign reading 'I am a mental patient.' You have not yet commented on my wish to control your fantasies. I thought you would have jumped on that like a dog on a bone."

"If a couple of glasses of champagne make you so eager for my opinions, I may provide the drinks myself on a weekly basis," he said, smiling at her. "First of all, remember *you* are the one who suggested that you were being unfeminine and aggressive in wishing to control my fantasies. Actually I don't think there is anything particularly unfeminine about your wish.

"Furthermore," he said, "I don't believe that you are unfeminine when you get loud and angry and demanding, with me or with your husband. You know, both little boys and little girls are loud and demanding, and usually the only reason they carry through with this behavior when they grow up is if they get pushed into a role that doesn't really fit. Certainly your mother—and maybe your father, too— helped you to believe that a real woman always defers to the man, is always cooperative, subservient, understanding, and accepting; never is she selfish, opinionated, competitive, and uncompromising. In real life with real people this formula doesn't work."

"Bravo!" Helen said and lifted her champagne glass in the air. "If there were a few more like you, women's lib would be out of business. Unfortunately, I don't think most men, probably even most women, agree with you. Society in general still expects us to behave in orthodox fashion—which essentially means staying at home and keeping our mouths shut."

"Well, I guess if you insist on letting conventional society dictate your behavior, you deserve the consequences. Be a true woman and suffer."

"Now, damn it, you're ruining my party, you bastard. First of all, I don't let conventional society dictate to me. At least not entirely. If that were true, I'd be at home scrubbing my floors so when the lord and master blesses me with his presence he wouldn't get the soles of his shoes dirty. At least I have enough ambition to hold down a job and keep a house, too. I don't know many men who could manage it." She gulped the remainder of her champagne and almost belligerently held out her empty glass for another. "You make me want to stand on your desk and shout that I can whip any man in the room," she said.

"Aha, now your true unfemininity is showing!" he said, refilling her glass.

"You really mean that, don't you?" she said.

"No, but I knew you'd have trouble in discriminating whether it was a joke or not."

"You are a bad guest, and I'm not sure I'll ever give you another party," she said, but she had relaxed in her chair once more and no longer seemed ready to challenge him to physical combat.

"I suppose I want to prove that you're still pretty touchy and that your husband could easily manipulate you into doing what he wants you to do by attacking your femininity."

"I suppose that's exactly what happens," she answered, pondering the thought. "Let me give you a for instance and you tell me if this is what you mean. Okay?"

"Agreed," he answered.

"I can go for long periods of time picking up Steve's dirty socks and the kids' books and vacuuming and doing all sorts of drudge-type chores and not complain or be bitchy about them, and I have to admit that during these spells I really don't mind them too bad. I think the reason I don't mind is because I think of these duties as necessary chores to do in between my job at the office, which I do find quite interesting and challenging most of the time.

"Then all of a sudden Steven will make some un-reasonable request—at least it seems unreasonable to me—like would I bring him a glass of iced tea while he is lying on the sofa watching TV and I'm still in the kitchen cleaning up from dinner. *That* literally blows my mind. I mean, the request itself isn't so unreasonable but his timing and the circum-stances are.

"So I fly into a rage and scream about how I have worked all day just as he has, and how I am tired, too, and why the hell can't he get his own goddamn tea. He gets that martyr look of his, slowly and pain-fully arises from his horizontal position and labori-ously goes and gets his own tea.

"He doesn't even have to say anything about what a poor wife I am, and how I won't even do what little he asks of me. He doesn't have to, but he usually does. He remarks 'how unladylike I am' and 'what dainty, womanly language I use' and 'how nice and wifely I am.' "

"Now if I could just go on being madder than hell at him, I'd be fine. But instead of staying mad, I immediately feel guilty. Secretly I agree with most of what he is saying, that it isn't really so terribly much for a man to ask his wife to wait on him a little bit, and that I truly am unfeminine and unladylike. It's enough to put me back quietly into the drudge routine for another spell and play the female role again until the next explosion."

"In other words," he said, "you are still a slave

to your early day image of what a woman should be."

"I might add it makes me a slave in more ways than one," she said.

"Doesn't it make you wonder how to get out of this role you have cast yourself in?" he asked.

"Hell, yes," she answered, "but I think it was type casting. It makes me wonder how to change my type. I suppose I naturally think Steve is at least half to blame, and I sometimes wonder if I wouldn't behave differently with another man. I mean if I were married to a wealthy tycoon, say, who provided me with jewels and servants and all I had to do was lie on my chaise all day and read French novels and eat bonbons, I don't suppose I'd mind very much if the poor tired fellow wanted me to get him a glass of iced tea after spending a long, hard day investing his millions. I think then I'd feel pretty darned unwifely if I didn't provide it before he asked. Do you see what I mean?"

"I see what you mean," he said. "You are telling me that it would be easier to stay in your narrow role of a female if you were well paid—and I don't mean monetarily—by a man who would stick to the stereotyped masculine role. I do believe that you think it might be easier to exchange men than to change yourself. Before you try to substitute a new man, I think you owe it to yourself to redefine your own role and become comfortable about it."

"Right now I think I owe it to myself to change the subject. This is far too serious a discussion for a party. Aren't you even interested in what is in the other box which I so prettily wrapped with my own two hands, my own two womanly hands?" she said, displaying her dimples.

He picked up the package and began to unwrap it. He was thinking rapidly about what direction to take. He could stay in the role of the therapist analyzing the gift of the patient or accept the situation as a good friend giving him a straightforward Christmas present.

Patients had often presented him with gifts in the past, some of them innocuous and some loaded with hidden meaning. He had learned that quite often the gift was not as important as the reason for giving it. Once he had received a set of inexpensive cuff links from a male patient at Christmas time. He and the patient spent their next three sessions trying to uncover and analyze the covert motivation for the gift. At the end of his therapy, the patient had wryly reflected on the ninety dollar cuff links he had earlier presented to his therapist.

Another patient, a young woman who had struggled for a long time with obsessive suicidal preoccupation, at the turning point in her treatment gave to Dr. Odell a gift wrapped box containing her hoard of sleeping pills. It was a gift he fondly remembered.

On another occasion a young schizophrenic girl with whom he had found communication impossible and who had found it out of the question to confide in or talk to anyone had finally brought to him as a gift a crushed moth. Through careful and gentle

questions, he was able to learn that she was in effect
showing him how she felt because she could not tell
him. She, too, felt crushed and dead. When he had
understood the meaning of her gift, he was able to tell
her that he could do nothing for the moth but that
together they could bring her back into the human
feeling world. The gift of the dead moth had been one
of the most significant factors in her treatment.

All these remembered incidents went through
his mind as he removed the bright wrapping paper
from Helen's gift. His final thought was, "Hell with
it, I'll play it straight. I won't analyze it."

"What's the matter?" Helen asked, quick to
pick up on any hesitation on Dr. Odell's part. "It's
not a viper, you know. And it won't jump out at you.
You look positively frightened to take the lid off."
(Oh, God, I've broken some unspoken rule in bringing him a present and he doesn't know how to tell
me.)

"I'm sorry. I got momentarily preoccupied with
some past gifts I have received, some of which were
strange to say the least."

"Well, sir," she said with an innocent wide-
eyed smile, "you have to keep in mind the type of
people you deal with. What have your patients given
you in the past, live hornets' nests? You truly need
have no fears if that is what is preventing you from
opening my present." (I'll bet somebody gave him a
snake!)

He laughed. "No, no hornets' nests, but one nice
lady gave me a book on etiquette once with the obvi-

ous intent that I should improve my manners," he said, lifting the lid of the box.

Inside was a putter with a retractable handle and a cup, an apparatus designed for practicing putting indoors. Packed around it were several dozen homemade Christmas cookies.

"How very nice," he said. "I must say I prefer to practice putting in my office to improving my manners. Thank you very much."

"You are most welcome," she said. "Actually it is not totally an altruistic gift. It is another conniving way of getting more for my money. You see, now when you have an empty hour in your appointment book, perhaps you will spend the time putting in here. And each time you do, you will necessarily think of me. The putter takes the place of my letters." She smiled, but they both knew there was truth in her reasoning.

"That sounds like a fair exchange. Does that mean I can blame you every time I miss a putt?"

"Certainly not. Only when you make it," she answered. "I only want you to have good thoughts about me."

"Well, you've brought me something to drink, something to eat, and something to play with. You're becoming very considerate about my pleasures. What would you call a bad thought about you?"

"I guess we'd have to define our terms first. I'm afraid I have never shed my rather idealistic views about 'good' and 'bad.' But the truth is—when you asked me about a bad thought about me just now—

immediately it came to mind perhaps you meant a sexy thought. There! Three glasses of champagne and I've uncovered a fundamental idea. Bad equals sexy. Now it's up to you to react as either a therapist or a man." She said it in a teasing, cocktail-party fashion, but nonetheless the challenge was there.

Dr. Odell felt that for Helen to initiate the subject of sex was an improvement, even if in so doing she accused him of bringing up the topic. He sensed that she was not ready for a frank, direct discussion of her sexual feelings, but that she was willing to approach the subject in an indirect way. It was obvious from her manner that she had been entertaining sexual fantasies about him but was reluctant to bring them into the open. He decided once again he would "model" for her the way he did on the day he expressed anger.

"One more drink of champagne and I might tell you one of my fantasies about you—if you promise not to molest me," he began. He could see he had taken the correct approach for Helen looked interested and receptive. "As I think about it, however, it certainly seems more like a good thought than a bad thought."

"Then by all means let's use your definition," she laughed. "Would you like me to lie on your couch while you tell me?"

"I'm surprised you'd even mention that couch," he said. "But stop interrupting me. I might forget that pleasant fantasy I was going to tell you." He had to think quickly in order to come up with a legitimate but safe fantasy which she could tolerate, one which had some romantic quality rather than being blatantly erotic.

"Remember the day you came here after lying by the pool all afternoon drinking Margaritas?" he asked.

"I certainly do—with great embarrassment, I might add."

"Stop interrupting me. This is my fantasy," he said. "Even though you felt awkward, you did look very cute and I was still feeling turned on when I left the office to go home.

"The fantasy started when I saw an elegant old Rolls-Royce limousine parked in the parking lot, and I remembered your affection for your big Lincoln. I could visualize you and me in the back seat of the Rolls being driven by a chauffeur wearing side blinders. It was easy to imagine that this elegant automobile had stereo and a bar and silk shades which could be drawn over the windows to give complete privacy.

"I really didn't care where we were going, but we seemed to be headed in the direction of Mexico toward my suddenly acquired yacht moored just off a private beach of white sand at Mazatlan. I say 'suddenly acquired' because I had acquired it in my head just that moment. I knew we really couldn't wait to make love until we got on the yacht, but it seemed as if we should be headed someplace."

"As of this moment I am switching from cham-

pagne back to Margaritas if they inspire this sort of
daydreams. I'm sorry. I know. Don't interrupt you."
She sat back in her chair eager to hear the rest of his
reverie.

"Having a practical bent and being a bit fumble-
fingered, I did put silent zippers and easy-to-unsnap
fasteners on all your clothes." They laughed together
at this admission.

"Once on the yacht—where we arrived exactly
as the sun was setting into the water, naturally—I
wasn't able to imagine your initiating anything very
lurid but you were admirably cooperative.

"I regret I may have left out a few details, but
until we have had more experience in talking about
sex, I think I'd better let you fill in the blanks with
your own imagination."

He had tried to tell her enough to let her know
that men do have these private wishes without necessarily carrying them out. He hoped it might enable
her to follow the pattern and also that she might feel
closer to him and more trusting since he was able to
openly admit a private fantasy of his own. Perhaps
she would even realize that this kind of intimacy
might cause him to like and respect her more rather
than less which was her usual expectation.

"Ah, shucks. Just when it was getting good,"
Helen said smiling.

"Good! I thought you said that sort of stuff was
bad," Dr. Odell said mildly.

"Not when you add certain ingredients like a
Rolls-Royce and yachts. And also so long as you

keep it all in your head like that. Also I found it very flattering. I wish my husband would have such day-dreams about me. Hell, I wish I had such daydreams myself!" (I wonder if he really had such a fantasy. About me! Or if he tells all his female patients the same daydream. He must think about sex all the time.)

"And I was hoping you might reciprocate in some small way for my sharing that daydream with you," he said. "However, I'm willing to wait. I really don't want you to share anything with me until you're ready."

"Oh, it isn't that I'm not ready," she said. "It is truly that I don't have such sexy fantasies. Well, that's not quite true either. I mean I start them. I just don't seem to be able to finish them. I have even started them about you, but somehow I always turn off be-fore, well before anything noteworthy occurs. I have always thought it was because I was afraid you would ask me about them and I didn't want to have anything to tell you because it would embarrass me. Mind you, it doesn't embarrass me to discuss sex in general with you. I could tell you really blue jokes without batting an eye. But that, you must agree, is entirely different from telling you my sexual feelings about you specifically."

She thought for a moment before adding, "I have had a couple of sexy dreams about you. I guess that's safer to admit because I don't have to claim so much responsibility for them. Dreams just happen, you know; you don't have any control over them."

"I wondered if you'd been holding out on me.

But I won't chastise you for that now. Have a little more champagne and tell me about your dreams." He emptied the bottle into her glass.

"Well, actually this one isn't very sexy. I've meant to tell you about it before but it seemed so pointless. But I'll start with it and see if you react appropriately and work my way up, okay?"

"I'm afraid to say anything for fear I'll give you reason to think I'm not reacting appropriately."

"Oh, don't be so touchy, Doctor," she said, mocking his oft-repeated words to her. "I dreamed I had missed several appointments with you because you had been out of town. On this day I was so delighted that you were back, I came running into the office bubbling and happy to see you after your absence.

"Everything about your office was the same as usual—except the couch was covered with a leopard skin bedspread of some sort. I never quite figured that part out. Anyway I was glad to see you and I ran to you and threw my arms around your neck and kissed you. Demurely on the cheek yet. Pretty sexy, huh?

"I was starting to tell you I had missed you and had so much to tell you about when this woman—I don't know who she was because she was faceless, but I seemed to think it was your wife—this woman burst into your office and began throwing apples at us. Apples! It made me very angry because I knew she was misinterpreting the embrace, which was purely platonic. Even so, she made me feel guilty, although I knew I had done nothing wrong and had not even intended to.

"When I woke up I associated the apples with Adam and Eve and the Garden of Eden, but the rest of it seemed pretty silly to me. What do you make of it?"

"Well, that leopard skin bedspread sounds pretty suggestive to me." He hoped he might be able to persuade her to claim her sexual feelings about the dream.

"Oh, that. That didn't seem to have any part in it at all. What I want to know about is the apples. Now if it had been stones or rotten eggs, I'd have understood it. But apples?"

"From your remark about Adam and Eve, it seems you do see the apples as some sort of temptation," Dr. Odell said.

"Except that I immediately dismissed it because it didn't make sense. Particularly as I had the idea that the woman who threw them at us was your wife. Because that would mean that your wife was throwing temptation at us. No, I tend to discount that theory." She sipped the last drop from her glass and looked with disappointment at the empty bottle. (Next time I'll bring a magnum. I do much better in here with some liquid support.)

"You said it was a faceless woman. You thought of her as my wife, but could it be someone else?"

"How would I know if she was faceless? I have never seen your wife, so I couldn't put a face on her if

I wanted to. That's one of the reasons I thought it was your wife." (Who the hell else do you think it could be? I'll bet he's working on that mother angle again.)

"Let me ask you this," he said. "Suppose you had been alone with me in this room with a couch covered in leopard skin and your arms around my neck and the woman had not come in. What do you suppose might have happened?"

"I get the message," Helen said, and for the first time during the hour she blushed. "I do believe I just admitted to having a sexy dream about you that I hadn't even realized was sexy and threw a faceless woman in to be my conscience. Just like my fantasies —I can't let myself finish them."

"Maybe you and I could finish them together," he suggested.

"It's interesting that you should suggest that," she said. "I was thinking how I was able to complete *your* fantasy a few minutes ago. In a few seconds I knew everything that happened on that yacht of yours.

"Maybe," she said, "it's because I don't have enough reality on which to base a good sexual fantasy. You know, sex is not one of Steve's most imaginative endeavors. In bed he behaves very much like a little boy at dancing class. He is taught certain steps and the order in which to take them; but if the little girl tries to change a step or embellish the dance, the little boy either has to start all over or quit. Choreography is everything. That is how my sex life is—always the same with no variation. So no wonder I can't finish my fantasies."

"I don't think you can entirely blame Steve and his lack of imagination. He is not your only source of fantasy. You once told me you read lusty books. Can't you use them as a basis for daydreaming?"

"Actually, I believe I prefer to finish your fantasies than think of one of my own. You do lead a pretty riotous life in your head, don't you?"

"Yes, but not just about sex though. One of these days we'll exchange sadistic fantasies."

"Okay. I'll bone up on de Sade for the occasion," she said.

"I realize it's about time for you to go, but I am reminded of a question I have meant to ask you for a long time. What was your initial attraction to Steve?" This question had been lurking in the back of his mind ever since his session with Helen's husband. He saw Helen as a very attractive and sexy woman, and it puzzled him to think that she would choose a man so much for security rather than excitement.

Helen looked absolutely blank for a moment. "After fifteen years of marriage, you'll have to forgive me if I have to stop and think a second," she said. "I suppose if I had to come up with a single adjective to describe Steve's attraction when we were dating I would have to say 'dependable.' Now don't laugh. I really did see him as the most dependable, responsible man I knew at the time. Ironic, isn't it, that it should turn out he is the opposite and what he was looking for was someone on whom he could depend.

"I remember early in our marriage when I began to discover this fact. At first when he shirked responsibility, it made me nervous. When there was a decision to be made or an unpaid bill worrying us, we would try to outwait each other. Gradually I would go ahead and take care of whatever it was because it worried me more than it did him. Eventually it became habit. I don't even think about asking him anymore to help with the budget or call about getting the roof repaired or whatever the problem is. I just take care of it myself. And we both know I will!

"Back to your original question," she said with a note of sarcasm directed toward herself. "I was attracted to Steve because I thought he would take care of me." She began to pack the crystal glasses back into their tissue-lined box.

"You have made it clear that you married for security rather than excitement," he said. "Even though you're tempted to follow the rigid thinking of your husband, I believe you can certainly create a sensational fantasy if you try. In fact, it's your homework to start and finish a really lascivious fantasy of your own. It can be about either me or some other equally attractive male," he said, "but I do want you to try to do this."

"If I do, will I have to tell you about it?" she asked.

"Not necessarily. You start a good daydream and finish it and then you can make the decision about whether or not you want to tell me about it."

"Okay." She grinned. "Is there going to be a test on this assignment?"

"Not as long as you can promise that you completed the assignment."

"Fair enough," she said, gathering up her purse and the box containing the glasses. "You know, it's odd. I momentarily had the idea of stealthily slinking out of here trying not to be seen. I almost feel as if I had been in here doing something illicit—on a yacht yet!"

"I really do appreciate your thoughtful gifts," Dr. Odell said as he went to the door with her. "I'm glad that you initiated a party today."

"Don't let the cookies make you so fat you don't fit into my extravagant fantasy now," she said.

"I'll have to hear the fantasy before I know how important my physique is," he said. "Have a Merry Christmas and I'll see you next year."

"Merry Christmas to you, too," she said. Her walk was jaunty as she swept gaily through the waiting room.

Chapter 15

Helen's Christmas party for Dr. Odell was a turning point in her therapy. For the next few months she began to make gradual but lasting changes in her thinking and her behavior.

During the spring she admitted to Dr. Odell that therapy no longer seemed so crucial to her. "For a long time," she told him, "it seemed that these hours with you were the only real hours in my life. It was the one time I allowed myself to genuinely think about how I felt, let alone to say anything about it. Once I left your office, I went right back to routinely shutting out bothersome or anxious thoughts and saving them for the next hour. Now I find I am able to really be myself at other times with other people."

"That's the whole point of what we're doing, you know," he said.

"All the same, it makes me a little nervous. What if I am not able to sustain it? I don't want to go back to living only a couple of hours a week."

Sustain her transition she did, however, and Dr.

Odell noted her progress in other ways. More than any other patient he had ever had, Helen had concentrated on her feelings toward her therapist. During the first year of her therapy, she connected nearly all her emotions with Dr. Odell. Almost never did she relate her present feelings and reactions to events in her past. Even in her letters the central theme had been her concern and speculation about either her own or Dr. Odell's feelings. She had mentally divided her life into two periods: before "scares" and after "scares." The period before her onset of anxiety seemed irrelevant to her. In dwelling on her feelings after she experienced anxiety, Dr. Odell became the leading character in her existence, either to blame or to praise. It was as if she had to experience and test every human emotion first with him before she could permit meaningful relationships with other people. Up to this time Helen had maintained she did not remember her childhood.

Once she began to relate the here-and-now to past events in her life, her memory of her earlier years became vivid. A consistent feature of her therapy was that, while she had often been late during the initial phase, she had never once missed a session. She came for her visits even when she had colds and the flu, once showing up with a temperature of 101. Furthermore, she had gone to work all day before her appointment.

When questioned about her resolve never to stay home sick, she told the doctor, "I am never convinced I am sick unless I am unconscious or there is

blood gushing from a wound. I always assume it is
just in my head. I am so afraid of being a hypochon-
driac that I have to have my family doctor order me to
bed before I can stay there without guilt."

Now, after over a year of therapy, she began to
see the reason for her attitude toward physical illness. She related to him a story of her childhood to
make her point.

"When I was a little girl," she said, "my mother
always worked, you know. She hated her job. I don't
blame her because it was damned hard work. She had
to be at that bakery every morning by six thirty and
nearly all year round it was dark when she left home.
She was always exhausted when she got home.

"As a child I seemed always to have a cold or an
earache or a sore throat. Sometimes I had to stay
home alone or with a grandparent, but when I was
about eight or ten my mother and I began playing a
little game. I gradually learned that if, during the
school week I mentioned that I didn't feel well, she
would immediately and without ceremony call her
boss and tell him I was sick and she had to stay home
with me. Then we would have a lovely time together,
listening to soap operas on the radio and drinking hot
tea. She would sometimes bake cookies and I can
remember she would go through the house humming
while I lay propped up in bed with coloring books or
paper dolls. They were the nicest days I had.

"However, if I happened to come down with
one of my ear or throat problems on a weekend her

response was one of disinterest or vague irritation. 'Oh, you're all right,' she'd tell me. 'It's just a little cold. Go play with your dolls and you'll forget all about it.' "

Dr. Odell, privately wondering how much Helen had let herself become aware of her mother's self-centered manipulativeness, said, "You had to be quite careful to choose the right day to be sick, didn't you?"

"Still do. The upshot of those years is that I still never quite know if I am sick or not. Particularly if I feel ill during the week, my first thought is that I don't want to go to the office and am making an excuse for myself. Once I have persuaded myself of that, I simply cannot allow myself to loll around in bed reading and pampering myself. A thermometer comes to my aid occasionally, because I feel it is an objective instrument and would not lie to me to get me out of work. If I find I do have a fever, I then allow myself to go to the doctor, and if he orders me to bed I can luxuriate in my viruses and germs without any guilt whatsoever. The point is somebody else always has to convince me I am really sick. My discrimination is impaired. I might add I have a hell of a good attendance record at work."

"What happens if one of your kids says he is sick?" Dr. Odell asked.

"Hmmm," Helen said, wrinkling her brow. "An interesting question." She pondered for a moment. "I suppose I am inclined to be the opposite of

Mother. Maybe too much so. Those kids have to be pretty convincing with their symptoms before I let them miss school.

"On the other hand, when they are undeniably ill, which usually isn't too difficult to tell, I do stay home with them. I must admit that I rather enjoy it, too. Perhaps part of it is remembering the days at home with my own mother. I think the difference lies in the fact that I don't hate my work and am not that eager to be absent. I simply like spending an occasional day with one child at a time. About the only time this happens is when one of them is sick. I suppose now you are going to inform me that I, too, am making illness too pleasant for my kids?"

"I really wasn't thinking that way at all. But I guess there's an element of truth in what you say," he said. "I have felt guilty because I haven't spent much time with my kids on a one-to-one basis. I wouldn't worry too much about it. Your kids probably pick up on the truth that their sickness is a happenstance rather than a main factor in your special attention."

"I hope so. I don't think I intend to change in that regard anyway. Myself, now, that's a different matter. I'll know that I am truly 'well' when I can allow myself to be 'sick.' Do you understand that at all?"

"Yes, I understand that. You, the only one who really knows, will be able to make an accurate judgment about your own degree of sickness."

Another area in which Helen made adjustments and improved her life was in the handling of money.

Financing her psychotherapy had been difficult since the beginning. When she fell behind in paying her fee, she either panicked and became certain that Dr. Odell would dismiss her or else she became angry and suggested that it was somehow his fault she was in arrears. This last accusation was based on her rationalization that he should have "cured" her by now, and since he hadn't, it was his own fault his bill was so high.

Dr. Odell instinctively knew that Helen could never accept the idea of a reduced fee. However, once during a tirade in which she spent an entire thirty dollar session wringing her hands in anguish about where she would get the thirty dollars, he did resignedly offer to negotiate for a lower fee. Her response was exactly as he had anticipated.

"What! And get less of your attention than anyone else! Hell, you'd feel you didn't have to apply yourself to my problems if you weren't getting as much money. You'd probably feel quite justified in spending part of my sessions writing letters to your mother. Then it would just take me that much longer to get out of here and wouldn't save either of us a dime. Hell, no. You just tell me if the bill gets behind too far. Then I'll have to quit. But as long as I am coming, I want your undivided attention—at the going rate."

Two weeks after this conversation, she marched triumphantly into Dr. Odell's office for her scheduled appointment with the announcement that she had partially solved her financial problem. She had given the matter considerable thought and had come up with an idea of how to make extra money. She was going to give piano lessons on Saturday afternoons and had already lined up four pupils. Her goal was eight pupils. She figured that eight half-hour lessons at four dollars a lesson would pay for an hour of therapy each week, about the amount she was falling behind. She was highly enthusiastic about her project because she felt she might regain her own interest in playing again. She had her piano tuned and started giving the lessons before she told Dr. Odell, because she wanted to be certain it was all worked out before she informed him of her plan.

A few months later she had eight regular piano students each Saturday afternoon and was thoroughly happy with her endeavor. Her own children, who had never expressed much interest in music before, now began to show signs of attraction to the piano and she soon had ten pupils. She dug into her old boxes of music books from college and began to practice on a regular basis herself—"to keep one step ahead of the kids," she remarked to the doctor—with the result that she regained a former source of enjoyment.

"I am no longer competing with the concert world," she told the doctor. "I now compete only with the way I played yesterday. It isn't nearly so demanding."

Within six months her bill with Dr. Odell was current. There was an additional benefit which she gained from her teaching, one that neither she or her doctor could have predicted. Helen had never formed many close relationships with other women. She had always worked and not found time for coffee klatches with her neighbors nor had she ever had a sense of missing anything because of her lack of female friends. Her piano teaching now brought her into contact with the mothers of her students, and she discovered that she was particularly drawn to two of these women.

The two ladies with whom she gradually became friends were near her own age with similar outlooks. Over a period of a few weeks they chatted after their children's lessons, and one, whose child was Helen's last student of the day, began to stay for coffee with Helen when she came to fetch her daughter. When this mother eventually invited Helen to lunch during the week, Helen found herself accepting immediately and making arrangements to be away from the office a little extra time.

Their acquaintance blossomed into a real friendship, and Helen was as surprised as she was pleased to rediscover that the company of other women could be fun. During her married life she had become so engrossed in her job and her family responsibility that she had gradually, without realizing it, neglected her female friends and grown away from them. Later, when she became aware that she simply had no women friends, she had excused herself on the basis that "most women are dull and boring," or "I don't have the time to gossip and play bridge that those

other women do." She had in the long run convinced
herself that she neither needed nor desired friends
of her own sex.

When she expressed these views to Dr. Odell, he
said, "If I voiced these same opinions, you would say
I was a male chauvinist pig."

Now that she had made two new friends, she
was eager to share her enthusiasm with Dr. Odell.
She said to him, "It's interesting because the very
arguments I used to make against women, their dull
conversation about kids and laundry, are the very
qualities I enjoy about Sue and Marge. We started
out, quite naturally, discussing their children's music
lessons, then our mutual children and their problems, and when we meet now our conversation is
almost exclusively female. And it is not dull. Quite
the contrary. In contrast to the routine and sameness
of life at the office, I am beginning to think that feeling like a real woman makes me much more flexible
and versatile."

"Let me go back to the first remark you made,"
Dr. Odell answered. "You said you saw women as
dull and gossipy and now you suddenly find them
stimulating company. What has made the difference?"

"I don't know the answer. I only know it has
happened and I am enjoying it. Do I really need to
know the answer in that case?"

"In this specific situation, you don't. But I
feel more comfortable when I can describe to myself
your change of attitude because I might be able to

help you apply it elsewhere in your life. Perhaps with your husband."

"I could certainly use some help there. While all the rest of my life is improving, my marriage seems to disintegrate more each day."

"Is there a connection?"

"Maybe. I think my new friends in a sense have replaced Steve. They are willing to share their private lives with me far more than he is. While he isn't willing to change and have a closer relationship with me, he seems to resent it when I turn to others for companionship. He shows his resentment by locking me out even more.

"Once I began therapy and learned with you how stimulating a real relationship can be, I wanted more of it. I know I began to demand more from Steve, more talking and sharing of intimate thoughts. The more I demanded the more he withdrew. In fact, he told me not long ago that I had become insufferable ever since I have been in therapy. He said it was a waste of time and money and had accomplished nothing except to make me dissatisfied with him. Whereupon he stomped off to meet his buddies for a drink."

"Could there be some truth to what he says?" Dr. Odell asked. "Is it possible that you have asked or demanded more in the way of emotional closeness so that it threatens Steve? Was Steve once closer to you and he has now pulled away, or is it that you have become more discriminating about what true closeness is?"

"I think it's a little of both. I think I have moved in closer on him and he in turn has retreated farther away. I am certain that when I openly express opinions or needs to him that I used to keep quiet about, it makes him very uncomfortable."

"Maybe your frank expressions are not so threatening to him as your pressure that he reciprocate and share his own feelings with you."

"You are probably right. All I know is that we seem to be at an impasse. I know several people who began psychotherapy for marital problems. Initially they seemed to be happier; then they got divorces. I truly don't want that to happen to me, I have fifteen years invested in this marriage. But I do know that what I have with Steve now is not enough. I just don't know what to do about it."

"It's too bad he keeps refusing to go to the marital groups," Dr. Odell said.

"He'll never go. He won't consider any type of therapy for himself. And do you know why? Because he is perfectly happy with things just the way they are—or were. When I was running the house and going to work and writing the checks and running the errands and not complaining too loudly, he was quite content. Now I'm doing chores but I'm bitching about it and demanding he share the responsibility and he doesn't like it.

"For example, several weeks ago I asked if he would take over giving the kids their allowances. I have always handled this, and the kids automatically come to me for their weekly sums or for any other funds they need. Steve grumbled about it but finally agreed to do it. The first week he didn't give it to them but gave them some excuse about not having change. When they came to me, I told them that they should take it up with their father who was going to pay them. Do you know he never did give those children a dime? After three weeks they both came to me explaining that they had been borrowing from their friends for lunch money. He had put me back in the same old position he always does—I can either do nothing and try to force him to do what he says he will, or I can once again step in and take over for him. Since the children were bound to suffer far more than he if I did nothing, I paid their allowances and have been doing so ever since. That is but one small example of many, but it sort of capsulizes our relationship."

"In this instance," Dr. Odell said, "I think you did the right thing. The kids would have taken the brunt of it otherwise. What about talking together more? Has that improved any with the two of you?"

"No. When he wants to have some really good human companionship, he goes out with the boys. While he is at home, he wants me to be there cleaning up the kitchen and putting the kids to bed. It seems to infuriate him that I'd want equal time with the boys and have the audacity to ask him to help with the chores so we'd have time to spend together. He looks at me as if I've lost my mind when I suggest it."

"Perhaps you are asking him at the wrong time and place. Maybe you aren't approaching him very diplomatically. You know, he probably isn't faking

his anger at your demands. If you say to him, 'I demand that you talk to me,' it isn't very likely he will
be able to.''

"There is some truth to what you say. I suppose
I have approached him like a Mack truck. This is true
especially on therapy days. I leave here all wound up
with ideas and want to discuss them with him and I
guess I go home expecting him to react in the way
you do. So I'll accept the blame for that part of it,''
she said.

"I do understand your position though,'' the
doctor said. "I think that what has happened is that
since your marriage you have changed a great deal
and Steve has changed very little. The reason you
changed was because you couldn't stand the relationship the way it was. You were uncomfortable with it
and Steve wasn't. He was quite happy the way things
were and saw no need for change.''

"What you say is accurate but doesn't help me
very much. As I see it I have three choices. I can
either go on the way we are, like roommates living
together only to share the rent. Or I can get a divorce
and hope for something better in the future. Neither
of those choices appeals to me. The only other alter-
native is for our marriage to improve. And I cannot
make it improve by myself, and Steve doesn't want to
because he sees no need for improvement.''

Helen's theme of discontent with her marriage
continued. Dr. Odell did encourage her to keep trying, but it was evident that Steve was becoming progressively more angry and threatened as Helen con-

tinued to make changes that were beneficial to her. Aside from her marital discord, Helen had made steady progress in recognizing and expressing her needs and feelings. Moreover, she was able to recognize and respond quickly and accurately to the needs and feelings of others. With her increasing awareness of Steve's maneuvering strategies, she became acutely conscious of other people's attempts to manipulate her, even when such attempts were those of well-intentioned friends. Her antennae literally vibrated if the attempts were not well intentioned or were done "for her own good."

She once told Dr. Odell, "At least half of the bad things that have happened to me in my life were done 'for my own good.' When I was little and wanted to learn to ride, I wasn't allowed to because my mother thought that to mount a horse was automatically to be thrown. To get into a swimming pool was a certain invitation to drown. To go ice skating was flirting with a broken leg. So I was never allowed to engage in any of these activities 'for my own good.' Nowadays when someone wants me to do something 'for my own good,' I automatically reject whatever it is."

During the spring Helen's parents came to spend their vacation at her home. For the first time Helen was able to enjoy their annual visit while seeing clearly also for the first time that they were people with many problems of their own. When Helen's mother attempted to take over in the kitchen, Helen was able to handle the situation. She either told her mother calmly that she had already planned the meal and would prefer that her mother rest and enjoy her vacation. If Helen was tired, she easily and gracefully relinquished the preparation of meals to her mother, had a drink with her dad, and allowed herself to be indulged and pampered without her former conviction that she was being forced out of her own kitchen. She confessed to Dr. Odell that while she was capable of maintaining this smooth relationship with her mother for two weeks, she did not feel she could have sustained it indefinitely. She felt her parents had enjoyed their vacation with her more than they ever had before, and was happy and pleased because of it.

When Helen and Dr. Odell compared her parents' visit this year with the prior year, Helen realized that she had gone through an irrational period of unduly blaming her mother and father for all of her problems and miseries. Previously she had managed to be artificially pleasant and superficially gracious to them during their visit, but now was sure that they had been as uncomfortable and tense as she had been.

As Helen was making subtle but steady improvement, Dr. Odell assisted in the background with encouragement and approval. In contrast with the older, more formal psychotherapy he openly showed his affection to her both in his acts and his words. Occasionally Helen would leave her appointment feeling quite upset over a remembered incident in the near or distant past. On these occasions Dr. Odell was very likely to put his arm around her shoulders and lead her to the door, giving physical comfort while saying, "It's all right, Helen. Remember, I do like you and I will be around if you want to call me. For tonight try to say the hell with it and enjoy yourself." With his reassurance, Helen was more and more often able to do just that.

In other ways he broke some of the old cardinal rules of psychoanalysis. Shortly after her success with her parents during their visit, a large bouquet of flowers was delivered to Helen at her home. She was amazed and then delighted when she read the card: "Congratulations to the new Helen, the grown-up daughter. Dr. Odell."

During an appointment when she had finally permitted herself to relate to him a detailed sexual fantasy, he gave her a bottle of French perfume, telling her, "This is to help remind yourself that you are a young, sexy woman with all the rights and privileges thereof." When she accepted the gift with a provocative smile, he said, "Now go home quickly before you put it on. I'm particularly vulnerable to that fragrance myself." Helen made a mental note to wear it to her next appointment. He was still the only man with whom she dared let her lusty feelings emerge to the surface without fear of consequences. She once told him that while she was physically chaste, at the end of therapy she would feel that she had had a wild love affair with him inside her head.

Once in the middle of her ultimate frustration with her marriage, Dr. Odell leaned over and took Helen's hand. He did it when he knew she was out of the reach of words. She was huddled over in her chair racked with sobs and he sensed only the warm touch of another human could penetrate her aloneness. She grasped his hand tightly and gratefully, her isolation slowly disappearing.

Sometimes Helen was inclined to get into a bad temper with very little provocation. At these times Dr. Odell was apt to nudge her with his foot and say, "How's your temper today?" Since his gestures were always keyed to the way he felt, they worked because the patient sensed his intention. The foot-nudging produced results. It brought enough humor into the situation that they could laugh together and then Helen could clearly say who and what she was angry about.

Each of these personal and special experiences served to cement their relationship. Dr. Odell did not plan or prearrange his gestures and his gifts to Helen or to any of his patients, but did allow them to happen when they came about as a consequence of his own involvement and responsiveness. The patients perceived that they were spontaneous and not contrived, and for this reason could accept them. The results were beneficial to both doctor and patient.

As August approached and Helen neared her second anniversary in psychotherapy, both she and Dr. Odell were aware that her therapy was nearing an end. While the very crux of her emotional problem, her marriage, had not improved, it was more clear in Helen's mind as to the nature of her conflicts with her husband and of the fixed roles in which she and Steve had cast each other. Therapy had given her sufficient insight into her marital strife that she did not feel entirely responsible for their difficulties. She was no longer threatened by anxiety each time an emotional crisis erupted at home, but was aware that both she and Steve would survive.

Chapter 16

Helen's tardiness and regression to her former hyperactivity were confusing to Dr. Odell on the day she forgot her appointment. Her steady improvement and progress had left him unprepared for her lateness, her flimsy excuses about car trouble, her flustered arrival, and her defensive behavior. While he was familiar with the phenomenon of patients experiencing a temporary regression and a return to old unsuccessful ways as they neared the end of treatment, he was never quite ready for it when it happened.

When Helen related the incident about Oscar Sampson and his little boy without having any real insight into her own feelings about the story, Dr. Odell speculated that just such a regression had taken place.

When she went on to tell him the episode in her early childhood about being left at home alone when she was sick and when she was able to see the correlation between her own feelings of rejection in that situation and the loving concern little Oscar had received, Dr. Odell did feel that congratulations were in order. After his congratulatory remark, however, he did decide to delve into the reasons behind her un-characteristic superficiality and her at-arms-length attitude early in the hour. In recent months she had become relaxed and emotionally intimate with him, and he was curious and concerned about her turning once again to the stilted manner of her very early therapy.

The fact that she had gradually emerged from her defensiveness during the hour encouraged him to con-front her about it.

"You've loosened up now," he said, "but you sure were uptight when you arrived today."

"That's a hell of a scientific word for a Ph.D.," she said. "Anyway you think I'm uptight if I don't either try to jump in your lap or have a screaming angry fit every session."

"That sounds a trifle bitchy, but it does sound more like you."

"It's a damned good thing you're a friend or I'd feel compelled to argue the point indefinitely," she answered. "However, I will admit to a fraction of bitchiness in my otherwise sunny disposition." She uncrossed her legs and stretched them in front of her, inhaling deeply on her cigarette as she slipped off her right shoe and wiggled her bare toes.

"Careful, I think your feet are sending messages again," he smiled.

"Oh, but you'll notice I no longer curl my toes,"

she said. "You know, there was a period of time when I left here every week with cramps in my legs from curling my toes so tightly in an effort to keep from letting feelings out." She now slipped off her other shoe and wiggled the toes of both feet. "Now, observe. They are wiggling; not curling." She smiled at him directly. "Only you would probably realize the significance of that."

"Now you sound like the Helen I have become accustomed to. I like you much better this way," he said.

"I'm glad you're around to remind me when I slip back into my rotten ways," she said. "Especially today. I think I know why I felt so flustered and behaved like a snot when I got here today. Remember when I used to be sure you wouldn't be here when I arrived? I had that feeling today. I wouldn't admit it to myself, but I know I was convinced you had deserted me. It seems silly now, but it's true."

"And I suppose you also began to imagine that I didn't like you and had just been stringing you along all this time?"

"You know me too well," she answered. "That's exactly how I felt. The worst part of it was the black hole of feeling worthless, unloved, and unlovable. Why should you be any different from the rest of the people I have dealt with this week?"

"It's been a long time since you have felt so bad. I know that you are strong enough now to handle almost any assault. What expert was working on you this week?"

"What expert always works on me?" she asked. "You know, Steve would have been a fantastic psychologist in reverse. I can come into a room where he is and be feeling marvelous and gay, and within two minutes flat I am convinced that the world is bleak and dreary and not worthwhile. And he's so damned cheerful himself while he's convincing me the world is a lousy place." She thought for a moment before adding, "It's not just Steve though. I have learned to tune him out enough not to let him get to me. It was Steve on top of a lot of other things. My mother and my daughter to be exact. Between the three of them, I was convinced that I must be such a witch that you, too, would reject me today. I suppose that's why I put on my you-can't-hurt-me armor for my appointment today."

"I have days like that myself," Dr. Odell said.

"Do you really?" Helen asked eagerly. "Do you honestly have periods where you feel vulnerable and everyone close to you is taking advantage of it?"

"Hell, yes. If I didn't have a few really good friends outside my family, there are lots of days I'd like to chuck it all and drop out of the human race." Dr. Odell was thinking of both his golf buddies and the loyal and devoted members of his countertransference group. These two separate sets of people, one social and the other professional, were extremely important in his life, and often served to replenish his drained resources. "I wouldn't let any of your patients hear you talking like that," she said. "It might tend to remove you from your pedestal."

"I have a terrible fear of heights anyway." He laughed, and she laughed with him.

"Actually the reverse might be true," she said. "Maybe it's good for your patients to hear you complain. When I've sat in this same chair crying and feeling hopeless, the last thing that helped me was your looking so calm and controlled and superior. On the other hand, when you have admitted to me some of your own fears or less noble emotions, I felt maybe there was a chance for me, too."

"What did happen this week that blew your mind?" he asked.

"Oh, a series of things, no one of which is a big deal. But I still have a tendency when one thing goes wrong, and then something else on top of it, for my mind to run on the theory that *everything* is going wrong. It's a snowballing effect.

"This low point began," she said, "when I noticed Valerie has been very withdrawn and moody lately. I can remember when I was fifteen too, and I know it's a terribly confusing age. I suppose her sulkiness has brought out both the mother and the witch in me, because I do worry about her and I'll admit I feel left out when I can't even get her to answer a question. Maybe I have relied too much recently on companionship with the kids, since Steve is angry with me most of the time.

"Anyway," she said, "Valerie has been moping and spending most of her time in her room listening to records and mooning over movie magazines. Yet the minute one of her girl friends shows up, she becomes vivacious and cheerful and the two of them closet themselves in her room and talk for hours. It does make me feel rejected. And jealous. It makes me feel as if all she needs me for anymore is to do her laundry."

"I'm sure it is harder to take because you and she were very good friends a short time ago," Dr. Odell said. "It is a good thing you have made some friends of your own, or you'd feel really out of it now that your daughter is growing up."

"If Valerie's teen-age idiosyncracies were the only thing, I think I could brush it aside," Helen said, "but while I was still feeling like an old bag with a daughter too grown up to talk to her mother, my *own* mother called me on the phone."

Dr. Odell remembered how well Helen and her parents had got along during their last visit and reminded Helen of her success.

"The last I remember," he said, "you felt happy and confident about your mother. What changed the picture?"

"A small thing indeed. As I say, nothing big has happened, just a lot of little incidents piled on one another. Mother called long distance just after Steve and I had had one of our interminable arguments. This one ended with Steve accusing me of being too expensive for him. Specifically his complaints were about the cost of my car, an unending lament on his part, and about the fee for my therapy. He ignores the fact that I pay for both of them and have augmented my salary at the office with the piano lessons on Saturdays. You'd think the money was coming right out of his pocket. He acts as if he is the old-fashioned head of the house earning the money and I am the silly little woman staying at home trying to spend it all.

"What really sent me bananas was when my mother agreed with him! Oh, she did it very subtly, suggesting that perhaps I should try to 'help Steve more by getting a smaller car' or 'give up my therapy because it is really a waste of time and money for a sensible girl like me.' I think the truth is she is embarrassed herself to have a daughter who sees a shrink." She paused for breath.

"By the time I finished talking to her, I felt like a small child who had been scolded for being selfish and foolishly extravagant and that Steve really was a long-suffering paragon of virtue to tolerate me." During this recital Helen remained calm but she watched Dr. Odell's face very carefully for the slightest hint in his expression which betrayed a hidden agreement with her mother's opinion.

"Don't look at me like that," Dr. Odell said, aware of her close observation. "You should know by now that I invariably differ with your mother. In the first place, I would guess that both your mother and your husband would consider it money well spent if I had persistently tried to push you back into your former role of being sweet, dutiful, overly responsible, and self-sacrificing.

"As to your car," he said, "remember we have discussed it many times. I agree with you that it was an impulsive, extravagant purchase. But I am also well aware that most of the time you function far too much as a thrifty, budgeting, self-sacrificing woman who places her family's needs above her own. When you step out of character, as you did when you bought the Lincoln, you terrify Steve and he thinks he must make every effort to get you back to 'normal.' As a side benefit, of course, he can use your guilt over your impulsive spending as a weapon on any issue. I guess you haven't given him any further ammunition since you've been in therapy, so he has used the car for two years to punish you, keep you in line, and divert any argument away from him back to you."

"Well, I'm damned sick of it," she said. "I have felt badgered and rejected by so many people recently. I'd like to trade in the whole lot. I feel as if I have a daughter who doesn't want me to be a mother, a husband who does, and a mother who wants me to be her little girl. At first it depressed me, but now it makes me madder than hell." She lit a cigarette and tossed the match into the ash tray.

"It's too bad I still have to have your permission to be mad," she said, exhaling smoke. "I wonder when I will be able to get through these episodes without you. Anyway, it does explain my feeling today that you wouldn't be here. I was prepared for total rejection from you, too. I am sure now that is why I forgot my appointment. It was my way of rejecting you before you could reject me." She smiled at him now. "I'm very glad you were here and that my boss reminded me to come today."

"I'm glad, too," Dr. Odell said. "But suppose I hadn't been here?" He knew he was putting Helen on the spot in asking her this question. He guessed that their relationship was stronger and more established than Helen realized. It was a question he would not have put to her six months earlier.

"I suppose my immediate reaction would be it was just what I had always expected," Helen said. "I would have felt like crucifying myself on your door and letting my blood drip on your carpet. However, once I got my masochistic rage out of my system, I am sure I would have called you and asked you where the hell you were when I needed you."

Well, I'll be damned, Dr. Odell thought. He was fairly certain that Helen had accurately described what she would have done, but he had never thought he would be able to get her to admit it.

"You mean," he said aloud, "you could actually forgive me for not being one hundred per cent reliable?"

"That's the reason I could forgive you, simply because you have been one hundred per cent reliable. Now, don't get smug and think you can begin being late or canceling my appointments," she said with a wry smile. "But during the last two years you have been the one dependable, consistent person in my life. I have been furious with you, confused by you and threatened by you, but I have never once felt that you did or said anything to me that wasn't in my best interest—or at least honest."

She squirmed in her chair now slightly self-consciously. "I guess what I am saying rather poorly is that I value my relationship with you. I don't want to lose it. I don't have a replacement. So I would not let it be ruined by a temporary lapse on your part. I might write my name in blood on your door, but I'd be back."

Dr. Odell laughed. "As long as it's your blood and not mine." In a more serious vein he said, "Do you realize you have just admitted you would dare to reach out first to me?"

"I think I would do it in safety," she said. "If you somehow disappointed me, I would be quite willing to stick around and listen to your explanation."

"I can even imagine you enjoying listening to my fumbling excuses of how I goofed."

Dr. Odell was experiencing the very pleasant and rewarding sensations a therapist feels when he reaches a genuine friendship with a patient.

"Of course I'd enjoy it! You've listened to enough of mine," she said. Her expression became solemn with her next statement. "I know it's about time to leave today, but I do want to mention one more thought I've had about forgetting my appointment and being snippy with you today. I'm aware that you have done about all for me that you can. I don't want to make therapy a lifetime project. I know that my main problem now is adjusting to Steve the way he is or leaving him. No one can make that decision for me." Her eyes became misty.

"The knowledge that my sessions with you are predictably ending makes me feel anxious and a little sad, but I know it has to be. I may have been feeling rejected by you today because I have been anticipating the end of therapy. I'll be leaving of my own accord, but I'll feel that you're throwing me out."

"I feel that I should break into your monologue," Dr. Odell said gently, "but you seem to be coming up with all the right questions and the right answers."

Even though he intellectually anticipated the end of Helen's therapy, he felt his first pang of regret as he thought of a permanent separation.

"When you do decide to leave," he said, "you know it doesn't have to be forever."

"I will hold onto that comforting thought," Helen said as she rose to leave. "Nonetheless, I am glad I'll be seeing you again on Thursday."

Her expression remained thoughtful and pensive as she walked slowly to the door.

Chapter 17

Helen's temporary depression lifted and did not return. She made halting but continuous plans to terminate therapy. Dr. Odell knew on the day that she initiated the subject, her actual departure was only a matter of time. She was dealing well with her feelings about ending therapy, alternately experiencing relief and apprehension and expressing them to the doctor. He, in turn, was glad she was ready to handle her life situation on her own, but he knew he would miss her. He felt regret and disappointment that he had not been more effective where Helen's marriage was concerned. During her last few weeks of therapy, Helen spent much of the time ruminating about the pros and cons of continuing or terminating her marriage.

It was late in October when Helen came for her last scheduled appointment. She was subdued and pensive when Dr. Odell greeted her in the waiting room.

Once seated in her accustomed chair, she said,

"I'm not going to spend my last hour in here blubber-
ing about leaving you. You've had your share of
tears from me already."

"It's hard for me to believe this is your last
hour," he said.

"For me, too. It's also my last chance to clearly
sort out where I stand with my husband. I know I
have reached the point where I have to make up my
mind. I also know I have to make the decision on my
own and stand by it. I don't think I can make such a
major decision until I have tried being around Steve
without the crutch of therapy. Maybe it doesn't make
much sense, but I need to know how I am going to feel
without you being around to support me every time
I have a marital crisis." Her voice weakened and Dr.
Odell knew that her tears were very near the surface.

"Besides," she said, "I know Steve has resented
my therapy and my reliance on you. It seems only
fair to him and to me, too, to find out if our marriage
will improve if I am not in therapy. I think he has
always harbored the suspicion that you and I were
two against one where he was concerned. Maybe if
you are out of the picture, he'll be more inclined to
make his maximum effort. I intend to."

"That sounds like a good plan to me," Dr. Odell
said. "Granted that Steve refuses any kind of therapy
for himself, I think your idea gives him the best
chance to make your marriage work."

"When I was young," Helen said, "I used to
have a system to help me make decisions. I'd head up
two columns on a piece of paper, 'For' and 'Against.'

Then I'd proceed to list every pro and con I could think of under the two columns. By the time I had finished, I had usually made my choice. I'm tempted to do the same thing now concerning my marriage."

"Maybe that is as good a way as any," the doctor said. "You want to try it out loud?"

"Okay. First the pros." She wrinkled her brow in thought. "I have seventeen years of my life invested with Steve. The idea of uprooting our lives and the children's would be very distressing. Steve is a good provider, and I do feel a certain amount of security with him. I mean he isn't likely to divorce me or run around with other women. He's interested in our house and making improvements. I would feel a little frightened, I am sure, at the idea of taking care of my-self and the children and giving up his financial support.

"On the other hand," she went on, "I am con-vinced that I will never really achieve emotional close-ness with him. You know, that delicious snuggled-down feeling of trust you have with someone you know loves you, too. I don't blame him as much as I used to for his inability to be intimate with me or share himself with me. I honestly believe he is as emotionally close to me as he can stand to be. On that score I must decide whether or not it is enough."

"I agree on your last point," Dr. Odell said. "Emotional intimacy with a true sharing of private thoughts and feelings is the ultimate in human rela-tionships and also the most difficult to achieve."

"That's certainly true enough," she said. "However, I am now aware that once having achieved it, it is nearly impossible to live without it. What frightens me today is knowing that I have come as close as I ever have in my life to feeling this way with you, and I might never see you again." Tears again filled her eyes but did not overflow.

"If it gets too lonely," he said, "call me and we'll talk about it. If it helps you at all, I do know that there are many people 'out there' who want emotional intimacy more than anything else, even if they can't really describe what they are seeking. Remember, there is always someone else who would like to laugh and cry with you and share his private and sometimes silly or stupid personal thoughts with you."

"I have wondered recently if I've been sending out invisible signals that I'd be interested," Helen said. "For years I have been efficient and businesslike and unnoticing of men around the office. Lately, I find myself looking at them more closely, watching for signs of interest, and occasionally wondering what they'd be like in bed."

"I had wondered when you might start thinking about or noticing attractive men," he said.

"Wonder no more," Helen said. "In fact, I have had lunch twice with one of the lawyers down the hall from Tom's offices. He is about my age, recently divorced, quite presentable and pleasant. I must admit I felt a little guilty even though both times were totally innocent. It's just such a change for me as I've not done this sort of thing before. I haven't told Steve about it, and I'm not sure why. I don't think I could ever feel serious about this man, but he is pleasant company. It was a pleasure for a handsome man to want to spend time with me and to talk to me and to be genuinely interested in my ideas and what I had to say. It made me feel good to be invited to lunch by him. It's the first time in a long while I've felt other than a mother or a servant."

"I wonder why you say you could never feel serious about this man," Dr. Odell said. "I don't believe you've ever mentioned him before."

"Nothing mentionable has ever occurred before," Helen said. "He has been in the building as long as I can remember, and we have nodded in the hall and in the coffee shop. In fact, he has invited me to lunch on several occasions over the past six months or so, but I just wasn't interested and really forgot about it."

"Hmmm," Dr. Odell said. "Any more of these admirers hanging around you haven't told me about?"

"Why, there's one behind every bush, don't you know?" Helen said. "You almost sound jealous."

"I think you're right," he said. "I guess I do feel as if I have helped groom you to be a really first-class woman. I'm human enough to wish there were some way to take advantage of it. Now some strange and undeserving man is going to come along and enjoy you, the lucky bastard."

"Oh, my God," Helen said. "You are worse than a father. I have gone to lunch with a casual acquaintance twice and you already have me indulging in a wild, illicit love affair with him. What you are doing, you know, is putting ideas in my head that weren't there before."

He rolled his eyes heavenward. "You're becoming a virgin again," he said, shaking his head. "At least you're claiming a virginal mind. I know you far too well for that. It's a little late for that claim, and it's also a little late for you to cast me in the father role."

"Perhaps you'd like to run away with me then and save me from all these alleged Lochinvars who are out to destroy my virtue," she said. "Do you have your Rolls-Royce handy?" (I would never have been able to say that until today for fear he would either reject me or take me up on it.)

"It's a tempting invitation," he said. "But I do have a prior commitment."

"Now it's my turn to feel a little jealous."

"Maybe that brings us back to our position of equality," he said. "We're both jealous but we aren't going to do anything about it."

"I guess I should spend what's left of my hour trying to figure out what I am going to do then," Helen said. She was serious now. "What I would like most is to have a successful and happy marriage with all the benefits that phrase implies. I would like to have it with Steve. I think I uttered a phrase almost identical to that when I first came to see you. Yet my marriage isn't much different than it was then. It's worse if anything, because now I'm more aware of what it could be. And Steve isn't. I think Steve would be totally happy if I quit therapy, went right back to behaving the way I used to, and didn't expect any change in him for the rest of his life. However, I no longer feel so apologetic about my needs and I'm able to state them outright. I vainly but persistently keep hoping that Steve will experience just a taste of the real joy of emotional closeness so that he will want more of it."

"You and I are both optimists. And if he doesn't?" Dr. Odell asked.

"Then I will have to learn to live with him as he is or leave him," she said. "Or take a lover." She smiled. "But I don't seem to have the necessary aptitude for a double life. I'd love to have a man to talk to who would relate to me, but if it began to progress beyond that point into an actual affair, I'm afraid I couldn't handle it."

"Maybe you couldn't," Dr. Odell said. "On the other hand, it's possible that you could. Your luncheon date with this man at the office suggests that you have broken the old pattern of blind loyalty. By blind loyalty, I mean being loyal to your husband because he is your husband rather than how you feel about him. I do believe that it would be hard for you to lead a split life in terms of an emotional and sexual life with one man and a domestic and family existence with another."

"That's exactly what I meant," Helen said. "I'm afraid in this area I am still pretty much of a square."

"Most of our generation is," Dr. Odell said. "I myself have felt envious of several of my patients who are in their early twenties. They don't seem to have the sexual hangups of our age group so they don't confuse sexual relations with emotional closeness."

"I'm not sure whether that's good or bad in the long run," Helen said. "Anyway I was born twenty years too soon to be liberated as the kids are today."

"I believe you actually have been liberated, and I'll be most curious to know the long range consequences," he said. "You know by now that I'm a very inquisitive man. If you don't call me and let me know about your decision, I'll call you."

"I'm sure I'll be in to talk with you once I decide. I have to admit though it's a marvelous feeling of relief to me to feel confident enough of myself to choose on my own which course to take. There was a period of time not so long ago when I didn't feel capable of selecting as much as an eyebrow pencil without depending on your advice."

"And now you're independently going off to make a permanent decision about your husband," he said.

"I suppose part of my confidence stems from no longer feeling that my decision is a life-and-death matter," she said. "Somehow I am able to face the future more calmly because I feel that I am going to succeed whether or not my marriage does.

"I have a friend," she said, "whose marriage was deteriorating. She confided in me that she was thinking of a divorce. However, she said she didn't want to leave her husband when the marriage was at its worst because she would always wonder if she had given up too soon. She stayed for six months after that and put all her effort into making the marriage work. She and her husband attended marital groups, therapy, they took a vacation without their children, and each of them tried to renew the marriage by finding out what particularly annoyed the other and ceasing to do it. And at the end of six months, she told me she thought her marriage was better than it had been in years but that it was not good enough. She left her husband when everyone thought they were having a second honeymoon. She later told me she was very happy she had waited to leave until their marriage was as good as possible. When that wasn't satisfactory, even if it could have been sustained, she was able to admit she had made a mistake and she left."

"A brave woman," Dr. Odell said. "I can't help but wonder if you are thinking of following her path."

"Perhaps. I would certainly be willing to give all of myself, but I can't do it unless Steve will help. There is a great difference between really trying and going through the motions. If Steve becomes more interested in working out our conflicts than he is in placing the blame for them, we might have a chance. I was such a devoted student myself at trying to fix the blame that I think I will be able to tell if he has changed."

"Without thinking too much about it, Helen," he said, "what changes in yourself are you most aware of?"

She pondered this question for a moment and lit a cigarette before answering. "I guess the most important one is that I have learned to trust someone completely—you. I almost automatically answered that the greatest gain from therapy was surviving anxiety and learning what caused it and how to cope with it. But you know I couldn't have done that if I hadn't learned to trust you and depend on you. You can't imagine what a great feeling it is to know that there is one person I can always talk to about whatever happens to me, good or bad.

"I suppose another important bit of knowledge I have acquired," she went on, "is that other people are just as scared and worried and anxious as I am and are searching, too, for someone in whom they can trust and confide. I think that since I have learned to trust you, I can more easily do so with some of those other people."

"I believe you can, too," he said. "You know, I have been attending a new kind of seminar recently. The professor insists on attention to the 'here and now.' All of this hour I have been persistently aware that I don't want you to leave. I would like to think of some pretext to have you come back for another hour and another. I guess I am saying that I care about you and I will miss you."

"Me, too," she said. "I'm not very good at good-bys." She wiped her eyes with the Kleenex Dr. Odell offered to her. With tears beginning to overflow, she said, "Are you sure you won't change your mind and run off to Mexico with me?" She put her cigarettes and matches into her purse and withdrew her dark glasses, preparing for departure.

"If I ever decide to run off to Mexico," he answered, "you'll be the first one I call."

"I'll hold you to that." She smiled through the tears.

"I suppose by the time that could happen though, you will have made your decision and be happily settled down, either with Steve or someone else. I can't imagine you without a man for long."

She rose and started to the door, then impulsively turned and hugged Dr. Odell tightly and kissed him on the cheek. He hugged her in return but before he could say anything, she murmured, "Thank you," and was gone out the door.

He walked slowly back to his desk where Helen's chart still lay open. He picked up a pencil and forced himself to write a final note.

"Case terminated regretfully. The last hour with a very favorite patient."

He closed the chart and with uncharacteristic efficiency filed it himself in his inactive drawer.

About the Authors

Harold E. McNeely, Ph.D.

Dr. McNeely is in private practice as a clinical psychologist in Phoenix, Arizona.

Past president of Maricopa County Clinical Psychologists, Dr. McNeely also holds memberships in the American Psychological Association, the Arizona State Psychological Association, and the Western Psychological Association. A diplomate in the American Board of Examiners in Professional Psychology, he is on the consulting staff of Camelback Hospital in Phoenix.

Dr. McNeely earned his doctorate in clinical psychology at the University of Nebraska. Married for twenty-two years, he and his wife have three children.

Norma Taylor Obele

In addition to her writing, Mrs. Obele is secretary to three neonatologists and transcribes for a firm of court reporters.

After attending Colorado College, Mrs. Obele traveled with her husband before they settled in Phoenix in 1960. For ten years she was a medical secretary to various psychiatrists, psychologists, and psychoanalysts. She has had nearly four years of personal psychotherapy.

Mrs. Obele is the mother of three children.